What THE Watchtower Society, *Doesn't* Want YOU TO Know

What THE Watchtower Society Doesn't Want YOU TO Know

WILBUR LINGLE

CLC PUBLICATIONS

Fort Washington, PA 19034

What the Watchtower Society Doesn't Want You to Know

Published by CLC Publications

ISBN: 978-0-87508-992-8
Copyright © 2009 Wilbur Lingle

U.S.A.
P.O. Box 1449, Fort Washington, PA 19034

GREAT BRITAIN
51 The Dean, Alresford, Hants. SO24 9BJ

AUSTRALIA
P.O. Box 2299, Strathpine, QLD 4500

NEW ZEALAND
10 MacArthur Street, Feilding

Unless otherwise noted, Scripture quotations marked KJV are from the *King James Version.*

Scripture quotations marked NIV are from the *New International Version*, copyright © 1973, 1978, 1984 by International Bible Society. Used by permission of Zondervan Bible Publishers.

Scripture quotations marked NWT are from the *New World Translation*, copyright 1961 by the Watchtower Bible and Tract Society.

The author has made every effort to be sure that excerpts from Watchtower publications have been quoted accurately, and that the only errors in style, grammar or punctuation are in the original.

This printing 2009

Printed in the United States of America

Contents

Foreword

One morning back in 1976 there was a knock at my door. At this time I was living in Japan, where I served as a missionary from 1954 to 1989. Little did I realize then what effect that knock would have on my life!

When I opened the door, I was greeted by two well-dressed Jehovah's Witnesses. They began by telling me about the awful moral conditions of this present world, then offered to explain how I could live in a "beautiful paradise" here on earth. This was less than a year after the Watchtower Society's prophesied date that the world would end (*October 1975*), to be followed by a "new world order."

These two Witnesses invited me to participate in a "Bible study" with them. Since I had read and heard various things about the Watchtower Society, I thought this might be a good opportunity to receive some clear answers to my questions. Instead of digging into books to learn more about the society, I assumed I could get the facts by talking to these two Witnesses. Since I am an inquisitive person and I knew my queries would require some time, I agreed to study with them *if* they would meet with me over a long enough period of time for my questions to be answered. They agreed.

I soon discovered that these two were quick to point out the faults of other people's religions, while at the same time arguing for the Watchtower Society's doctrine. In addition, they were expert at playing what I call "Bible ping-pong" (I quote one verse, then they quote another one back, without either of us really listening). Moreover, they clearly didn't like to answer thought-provoking questions concerning the organization. They either didn't know or didn't want to tell me about the history of the society, or about the men in the governing body of the society. I wanted to know, for example, where these men obtained their authority and how they received "guidance from God"—especially since they seemed to make so many mistakes!

When any particular Watchtower Society blunder was brought up for discussion, these Witnesses excused it by saying that the society was "making progress" by getting "new light." But when I asked where this new light came from—since it so often turned out to be "false light" and needed to be changed again in the future—they did not know.

As a result, after four meetings they did not return. I had always been taught to keep a promise. Breaking one is the same as telling a lie, which is a sin. But this didn't seem to bother them.

Well, those four sessions whetted my appetite. I wanted to find out more about the Watchtower Society. Since then I have spent thousands of hours researching the society and have compiled a library of most of the books and magazines published by them. What I have learned is firsthand and not from "apostate" material—which is what Jehovah's Witnesses call resources outside of their influence.

I have also conversed with many Witnesses since that

time, but they have ordinarily tried to avoid any questions about the organization—or have given merely perfunctory answers. Even the inquiries I have mailed to the society's headquarters have not resulted in clear and adequate answers.

My extensive research has prompted me to write this book, which I trust will enlighten you and help you discover *what the Watchtower Society doesn't want people to know!*

Have you ever wondered what it is like to grow up as a Jehovah's Witness? How does it feel, for example, to remain seated in school while your classmates salute the flag?

What is it like to live in constant fear of Jehovah God—worrying you will do something to displease Him or cause Him to annihilate you at death?

Why do so many Jehovah's Witnesses continually change Kingdom Halls, trying to find the love that is supposed to be universal among Witnesses?

Why do most Jehovah's Witnesses always seem so busy?

Why do 35% of Witnesses in America eventually leave the society—if, as the Watchtower Society claims, it is truly the most wonderful organization on earth?

Who really is the "faithful and discreet slave" (a name given to the Watchtower leaders)?

Does the Bible actually stipulate that blood transfusions are forbidden? Have the thousands and thousands of Jehovah's Witnesses who refused to accept blood truly pleased God—or have they died in vain?

Why does the society so often reverse itself, confusing its adherents?

Where is the true meaning of life to be found?

Did you know that the Watchtower Society tried to compromise with Hitler's Nazi regime by saying good things about it and praising its goals?

Did you know that the *New World Translation* of the Bible, produced by the Watchtower Society, still teaches that *Jesus is Jehovah,* which contradicts Watchtower doctrine?

Did you know that much of the society's so-called "new light" is only recycled "old light"?

These questions and many more will be thoroughly examined in *What the Watchtower Society Doesn't Want You to Know.*

Wilbur Lingle

Introduction

Often when Jehovah's Witnesses, or those studying with them, are presented with proof of the changes in the Watchtower Society's teachings and practices down through the years, they respond by saying, "You only want to find errors in its teachings; thus, you are not sincere, and I do not want to listen to you."

The Watchtower Society should permit the Jehovah's Witnesses to take the advice that it gives to others. There is a very interesting article in the June 22, 2000, *Awake* entitled "Do Not Be a Victim of Propaganda!" The article starts out by saying,

> There is a difference—a big difference—between education and propaganda. Education shows you *how* to think. Propaganda tells you *what* to think. Good educators present all sides of an issue and encourage discussion. Propagandists relentlessly force you to hear their view and discourage discussion. Often their real motives are not apparent. They sift the facts, exploiting the useful ones and concealing others. They also distort and twist facts, specializing in lies and half-truth. Your emotions, not your logical thinking abilities, are their target.

The article goes on to list ways to evaluate any message. It urges people "to scrutinize whatever is presented," to use the Bible as a guide so that "trustworthiness depends on the validity of the facts," and to ask questions. But I think this is the most challenging statement: "If possible, try to check the track record of those speaking. Are they known to speak the truth? . . . Why should you regard the person—or organization or publications . . . on the subject in question?"

But just let someone try to investigate the "track record" of the *Watchtower Society* and see what happens! Most of the Kingdom Halls have a rather extensive library of Watchtower publications, but they are only for show, not for reading. Permission from the elders must be obtained to read any of this material, and an elder must be present as the books are read. Those who ask about the older material will be questioned as to where they got the information about it and from then on will be looked upon with suspicion.

One example of this occurred in Spain. A very zealous and faithful Jehovah's Witness, who liked to be well-informed on the history of the society, heard that the Watchtower headquarters in Spain had a collection of old books that were not available in other Kingdom Halls. This man made arrangements to stay with a friend at the headquarters with the hope of being able to do some research in the library. But when he arrived, he found that these books were under lock and key, unavailable to the average Witness.

This was a big shock and disappointment to him, but it started him thinking: *What did the Watchtower Society have to hide in those books?* He then found out he could get the historical information he was looking for over the Internet. When he became aware of the many changes in Watchtower teachings over the years, as well as their unbiblical interpretations and false prophecies, he eventually decided to leave the society.

I have spent hundreds of hours investigating the Watchtower Society, and all that is presented here has been thoroughly researched and documented. The purpose of this book is to help you find out their track record without having to do all the research that I did.

Based on the Bible?

There is an important and challenging warning given in the 1982 Watchtower publication *You Can Live Forever in Paradise on Earth*. We read:

> Since many religions today are not doing God's will, we cannot simply assume that the teachings of the religious organization we are associated with are in agreement with God's Word. The mere fact that the Bible is used by a religion does not of itself prove that all the things it teaches and practices are in the Bible. It is important we ourselves examine whether they are or not. . . . The religion that is approved by God must agree in every way with the Bible; it will not accept certain parts of the Bible and reject other parts.

One of the first things that a Jehovah's Witness will tell you when you study with them is that *everything* the society teaches is based on the Bible. If this is really true, why don't they use just the Bible in their so-called "Bible studies" instead of Watchtower publications? Actually, the Watchtower Society uses only about six percent of the Bible in their publications and ignores the rest. I urge you to check what I have written with the Bible so that you can come into the truth.

A very sincere former Jehovah's Witness elder told me the following story. The elders in his area in England went away for a weekend of training. This elder was excited, because he was hoping to learn something to help him be a better elder. To his surprise the only training he received was on how to control the congregations, because "they could not be trusted."

But one thing they said stuck with him: "Never say, 'the Watchtower Society teaches thus and thus,' but always say, 'this is what the Bible teaches.'"

After this incident he was reading the Bible and noticed some things that did not agree with Watchtower teachings. This made him curious, so he started reading more of the Bible and comparing it with Watchtower literature. The more he read of the Bible, the more he realized that the Watchtower Society was not founded on the Bible, but on the words of men. He then stopped reading Watchtower literature and read only the Bible, and came to this realization: Salvation is not found in the Watchtower organization, but only in the precious blood of Christ that was shed on the cross.

The Bible gives us a clear warning that we should all take to heart. First Timothy 4:1 states that in the "later periods" (and the Watchtower Society teaches that we are living in this period of time) there will be many false prophets and teachers, and Second Peter 2:1 reveals that "many" will follow these false teachers. Since the Watchtower Society continually keeps boasting of its growth and its many followers, should we not be wary of such an organization and be willing to investigate it?

As you read this book consider the challenge given in the 1968 Watchtower publication *The Truth That Leads to Eternal Life*:

> We need to examine, not only what we personally believe, but also what is taught by any religious organization with which we may be associated. Are its teachings in full harmony with God's Word, or are they based on the traditions of men? If we are lovers of truth, there is nothing to fear from such an examination.

I would wholeheartedly agree. If you are a lover of the truth, you should have no fear of reading this book.

Chapter One

A Brief History of the Society

How did a religion as strict and as strange as the Watchtower Society originate? This is a question many people ask, and it deserves an answer. Does this religion go back to New Testament times? Can it be traced back to the 1500s, the time of the Protestant Reformation? Actually, no; it had its start in the late 1800s, and its adherents were initially known as "Bible Students" rather than Jehovah's Witnesses.

Many facets of the organization's history call for detailed scrutiny—and later we shall consider some of the "juicy details." But first, here is a quick overview that should prove helpful.

The founder of the Watchtower Society was Charles Taze Russell, born in 1852 in Pittsburgh, Pennsylvania. Though raised a Presbyterian, he eventually joined the Congregational Church, because he preferred its views. However, he was repulsed by some of the basic tenets of orthodox Christianity—particularly the doctrine that man's soul is immortal and eternal judgment awaits those who refuse to accept the salvation that Jesus Christ provides. For a period of time he strayed away from Christianity and even examined several Oriental religions. (Their influence is evident in some of his later writings.)

One evening in 1869 he attended a meeting at an Advent Christian church. The preacher, Jonas Wendell, expounded his church's belief that hell is not a place of punishment, but only "man's common grave." Finding this view in harmony with his own ideas, Russell started a small study group and began reinterpreting the Bible to fit this concept. This group eventually grew into the Watch Tower Bible and Tract Society.

The society uses the date 1874 as the actual beginning of the organization. In 1879 Russell published his first magazine, *Zion's Watch Tower*. The organization's first headquarters was in Pittsburgh, but in 1908 property was purchased in Brooklyn, New York, which is where the current headquarters is to this day and is often referred to as "Bethel." The people who work there are known as "Bethelites." Russell is mainly remembered for his prediction that the world would end in October 1914. He died in 1916.

The second president of the society was Joseph Rutherford. Born in Missouri in 1869, he went to college, studied law and became an attorney. In 1906 he was baptized as a "Bible Student" and a year later became the society's legal counsel. Rutherford was not in line to be the next president, but through a power struggle he was able to manipulate the election and became the second president in 1917. Rutherford was a domineering personality who tended to rule with an iron fist. While Russell was responsible for a lot of the basic teachings of the society, Rutherford was mainly responsible for the distinctive practices of the Witnesses: not observing holidays or birthdays, not going into the military, going from door to door, etc. He died in 1942.

Nathan Knorr became the third president of the society. Born in Bethlehem, Pennsylvania, in 1905, he was baptized at the age of eighteen in 1923. He went to the Brooklyn headquarters the following year. In 1940 he became the vice president and in 1942, at the age of 36, became president. Knorr was neither a theologian nor a writer, so from that time on the writers of the Watchtower books and magazines were no longer listed. Knorr was an organizer, and under his leadership the membership grew. He continued the practice of "one man rule," like Russell and Rutherford, until 1971. In that year a governing body was forced upon Knorr to avoid a rebellion. As a result, much of the power of the presidency was lost. Knorr died in 1977.

When the governing body was formed, it was clearly stated that its membership had to be from "the anointed," the 144,000 mentioned in Revelation 7:4. Only those of "the anointed," so the society claims, have the ability to interpret the Bible.

Frederick Franz became the fourth president. He was born in Covington, Kentucky, in 1893 and was baptized in 1913. He was then in his second year of college, but he never graduated. Instead, he left after his third year to become a full-time *colporteur*, a traveling Bible and religious book salesman. (This was in 1914, the year that Russell predicted Armageddon was to occur on October 1.) In 1920 he became part of the Bethel family in Brooklyn, New York. Franz became vice-president in 1945, and upon the death of Knorr took over the presidency in June 1977. Franz was more of a theologian than Knorr and predicted that the world would end around October 1975. He died in 1992, at the age of 99.

Upon the death of Franz, the governing body of the Watchtower Society chose Milton Henschel, 72, as the fifth president. He was a third-generation Jehovah's Witness in Pomona, New Jersey, and was baptized in 1934. He passed away in 2003.

In the year 2003 Don Adams became the president of Watchtower Society. He is not one of "the anointed."*

---

* Since the society teaches that only "the anointed" may be on the governing body, the organization has broken its own rules with the appointment of Adams as president. It was only a matter of time before this would happen, however, since the Watchtower declared in 1935 that the number of 144,000 was filled, and that those baptized after 1935 were not of "the anointed."

Chapter Two

Character of the Watchtower Leaders

Let us now take a closer look at the leaders of the Watchtower Society and see how the organization has been influenced by the character of these men.

Charles T. Russell

Charles Taze Russell borrowed most of his doctrinal ideas from other religious groups and taught many things that even the Watchtower Society now considers "pagan" and unbiblical.

In the 1993 publication *Jehovah's Witnesses— Proclaimers of God's Kingdom*, we read the following explanation of the society's inception:

> That meeting renewed young Russell's determination to search for Scriptural truth. It sent him back to his Bible with more eagerness than ever before. Russell soon came to believe that the time

was near for those who served the Lord to come to a clear knowledge of His purpose. So, in 1870, fired by enthusiasm, he and a few acquaintances in Pittsburgh and nearby Allegheny got together and formed a class for Bible study. According to a later associate of Russell, the small Bible class was conducted in this manner: "Someone would raise a question. They would discuss it. They would look up all related scriptures on the point and then, when they were satisfied on the harmony of these texts, they would finally state their conclusion and make a record of it." As Russell later acknowledged, the period "from 1870 to 1875 was a time of constant growth in grace and knowledge and love of God and his Word."

As they researched the Scriptures a number of things became clearer to these sincere truth seekers.

But if what the society teaches today is true, then Russell had no real authority to start a religious organization, or any way of properly understanding the Bible. The Watchtower Society now dogmatically teaches that the Bible *cannot* be understood on its own—that people need a Jehovah's Witness to teach them what the Bible really says. So how did Charles Russell become qualified to expound the Bible?

The Watchtower Society now teaches that the Bible is an "organizational" book—no individual can understand it on his own, but must be taught by the "governing body" of the Watchtower Society. What organization and governing body taught Russell? None.

The society further teaches that it is necessary to be baptized by immersion and be one of the "anointed," which enables them to receive God's Spirit, in order to interpret the Bible correctly. But we never read of Charles Russell being baptized. When was he anointed?

The society now translates the Greek word *presbuteron*— "elders"—as "older men." Did Charles Russell qualify as one of "the older men" when he founded the Watch Tower Bible and Tract Society at the age of twenty-two?

Russell had been greatly influenced by followers of William Miller (1782–1849), at that time called "Second Adventists," a movement which was a predecessor to the Seventh-Day Adventist Church. In their speculations concerning the return of Christ, the Millerites were prone to setting dates. They also denied a literal hell. Russell sided with the Millerites in his denial of any conscious punishment after death. But he didn't stop there. He also rejected the Trinity, the deity of Christ, the personality of the Holy Spirit and the immortality of the soul.

Russell is best known, however, for his incorrect prophecy that the world would end on October 1, 1914. Earlier it had been taught by some Second Adventists that Christ would return to set up His kingdom in 1874. When this did not occur, the teaching was revised to mean that Christ began reigning *invisibly* in heaven in 1874 but would bring a complete end to this old world's system forty years later—in 1914. (Russell borrowed the date 1914 from N. H. Barbour, an Adventist leader, but few people realize this because Russell never mentioned the source of his date.) He claimed that in 1914 Armageddon would occur, which would be the end of this present world system. When the world didn't end in 1914, Russell revised the date to 1918, but his death in 1916 prevented him from doing any further revisions.

Interestingly enough, a number of Russell's teachings are now considered "pagan" by his spiritual progeny. For example, Russell encouraged the celebration of Christmas and other holidays, along with birthdays. He taught that the Bible said nothing against a person serving in the military. He saw nothing wrong with blood transfusions. He taught that not only the 144,000, who are supposed to be "the bride of Christ," went to heaven, but all the members of the "great crowd" as well, even though the "great crowd" could not achieve the same position as those who were considered the "bride of Christ."

He believed that the Jewish nation would one day be revived, and the Jewish people would be the primary people to populate the new earth during the Millennium. He taught that the Great Pyramid stood as a testimony to God and believed the measurements of its "Grand Gallery" indicated the return of Christ in 1914. He taught that Christ died on "a cross" and not on "a torture stake." He completely rejected any kind of "organization" which is today considered absolutely necessary.

But let us consider a few of the boasts made about Charles Russell in the 1917 publication *The Finished Mystery.*

He [Pastor Russell] was eager to learn all he could about the Heavenly Father's will. It was not of himself that he learned and taught the Divine Plan: but God Himself caused him to learn, believe and teach. [p. 382]

The mind of Pastor Russell was filled with Truth. Crystal clear, and with hard, irresistible logic, the Present Truth, which constituted his wisdom and understanding was the hardest proposition ecclesiasticism ever encountered. [p. 383]

The Spirit raised Pastor Russell up to an understanding and appreciation of Heavenly things. . . . The mighty rushing sound represented Pastor Russell's receiving a rich endowment of the Spirit of God to whose leading he was fully consecrated and to whose influence and guidance he wholly devoted his life. [p. 384]

Many Christian ministers have had glimpses of the Word of God, knowledge of some details of the Plan, some measure of the Holy Spirit; but to Pastor Russell, God's messenger to the last stage of the Church, was given a superabundance of gifts, to set the things of God in order, to proclaim a harmonious understanding of all the Divine purposes of mankind and of some of the angels. [p. 385]

But of all the boasts this is probably the greatest:

The function of watchmanship was not given until 1881. Faithfulness in individual watching during a trial period of seven years was rewarded by the bestowal of the office [to] the greatest servant which the Church of God has had since the Apostle Paul. [p. 387]

But in what kind of condition was the Watchtower Society left at the time of Russell's death in 1916, after forty-two years of Bible study under his leadership? The following quotes are taken from Watchtower publications and not from any of the enemies of Russell.

When the Society began to be freed from further preaching work following World War I, they soon realized they had been held in spiritual bondage too in many ways. There were many false doctrines and practices that had not yet been cleaned out of the organization. Not all of them were recognized at once, but gradually over the years that followed it became evident to what extent the brothers had been in Babylonish captivity at that time. With considerable misunderstanding they had accepted earthly political governments as the "superior authorities" that God had ordained according to Romans 13:1; and as a result the Witnesses had been held in fear of man, particularly the civil rulers.

Besides, many were putting emphasis on so-called "character development," in the belief that there were certain saving qualities in their self merit, and there was considerable creature worship in the organization. Furthermore, such pagan holidays as Christmas were being celebrated, and even the symbol of the cross was used as a sign of Christian devotion. Also, although the name Jehovah was used from time to time, it was held in the background and its true significance not brought to light. Organizationally the Witnesses were still practicing the democratic style of local congregation government. In other words, it was a time of everyone's doing what was considered right in his own eyes, and the entire arrangement was a loose association without theocratic direction. The changeover in thinking had been so striking in many ways, from the 1870's down to 1918, that these tainted bonds of false conceptions and practices, inherited from pagan traditions adopted by Christendom, had slipped by unnoticed by the brothers. (*Jehovah's Witnesses in the Divine Purpose*, 1959, p. 91.)

This next quote from a Jehovah's Witness was included in the July 15, 1996, *Watchtower* magazine: "I am so thankful that I have lived in the knowledge of Jehovah's purposes from these early days just prior to 1914 when all was not so clear . . . to this day when the truth shines like the noonday sun." He said that after forty years of Charles Russell's teachings, things still weren't very clear.

H. Macmillan states in his book *Faith on the March* (1957):

And yet the knowledge of God's Word that was available to us at that time [Russell's era] was so limited (compared with what we now rejoice in) that it would be like coming out of the faint light of dawn into the brightness of high noon. But the gradual growth in knowledge, as well as in numbers of persons associated in the work, has strengthened and developed the organization and brought it to maturity.

Thus, it is admitted by the Watchtower Society itself that Charles Russell did not have a very good handle on interpreting Scripture correctly, that he borrowed a lot of doctrines and practices which later proved to be wrong and pagan, and worst of all, he did not understand prophetic Scripture or he would not have incorrectly predicted the end of the world on October 1, 1914. As a result, the Watchtower Society has spent many years attempting to sort out the truth about Charles Russell's teachings.

To this day it has not fully decided, because it constantly changes its teachings. If Russell and his followers had been led by God's Spirit to interpret the Bible correctly in the first place, they would have "the truth," and truth need not, and cannot, be corrected or changed.

Joseph Rutherford

Joseph Rutherford, the second president of the Watchtower organization, also put forth many false teachings and gave two false predictions about the end of the world.

In 1917 Joseph Rutherford succeeded Russell. He also followed Russell's pattern for setting dates for Christ's return. Initially he said it would occur in 1925. The net result of this prediction was a 44% increase in Watchtower membership. But when the world did not end in 1925, Rutherford revised his date to the early 1940s. Again the world did not end, and the prophecy was quietly ignored.

In addition to these false prophecies, Rutherford added to the confusion by putting forth many ideas that, later on, needed to be revised. In 1935 his greatest error, which was never rectified, was to divide Jehovah's Witnesses into two classes—the "bride" and the "great crowd." In 1931, Rutherford also claimed that the Bible forbade vaccinations. Strangely enough, Witnesses were suddenly permitted to receive vaccinations again in 1952.

In 1929, at the start of the Depression, Rutherford had a large mansion built in San Diego, California. He called it

"Beth-Sarim," House of the Princes. Rutherford explained that the Millennial Kingdom would soon be set up and God would send some of the Old Testament princes—among them Abel, Enoch, Noah, Abraham, Jacob, Joseph and Moses —to help Christ reign upon the earth. Beth-Sarim was deeded to these princes so that they might have a place to live when they came to earth.

Of course, the princes never appeared—but Rutherford made good use of it six months of the year. He also had two eight-cylinder Cadillacs that he rode around in. Beth-Sarim was sold following Rutherford's death in 1952.

One of Rutherford's directives that caused great suffering for male Jehovah's Witnesses was his stand on neutrality in November 1939. This meant that Jehovah's Witnesses were forbidden from going into the military, nor could they take "alternate service" instead of being drafted. Many Witnesses went to prison during World War II and the Vietnam War, because they refused to be drafted or accept alternate service. (I personally know a lady whose husband went to prison during World War II and whose son went to prison during the Vietnam War.) But in the May 1, 1996, issue of the *Watchtower*, all these directives were changed; Jehovah's Witnesses now can accept alternate service in place of the draft in countries where this is permitted. In the countries where it is not, the Witnesses are allowed to obey their government and go into the military.

Russell had taught that the term "superior authorities" mentioned in Romans 13:1 applied to earthly rulers. Therefore, governing authorities were to be obeyed. In 1929 Rutherford said the "superior authorities" applied to Jehovah God and Christ Jesus. He further said that the former interpretation was of the devil. Many Witnesses left the organization because they could not accept Rutherford's new interpretation. But strange as it might seem, in 1962 the society reverted back to Russell's interpretation of Romans 13:1—even though Rutherford had declared it was from the devil and had caused the Watchtower Society to go into "Babylonish captivity" in 1918.

Nathan Knorr and Fredrick Franz

Old habits never die—nor, in the case of the Watchtower, do they even fade away.

The misunderstanding of prophetic Scripture which caused Russell to declare the end of the world in 1914, and led Rutherford to prognosticate Armageddon for 1925 and, later, the early 1940s, did not stop the Watchtower Society from continuing to set dates.

In 1942 Nathan Knorr became president of the Watchtower Society, with Frederick Franz as its vice president. From 1967 Franz (who was the society's reigning theologian) promoted his theory in many Watchtower publications that man's 6,000-year reign would surely end in October 1975—at which point the Millennium would begin. And since the present world system must end before a new system can be constructed, Armageddon had to take place.

Most Witnesses believed their leaders' prophecy about 1975. Some sold their homes and businesses, and for a number of years lived off the proceeds, spending the years before 1975 going from door to door full-time, spreading the teachings of the Watchtower Society. The threat of Armageddon worked as a scare tactic, and Watchtower membership increased greatly from 1970 to 1975. But when Knorr's prophecy proved false, people were sorely disappointed!

Even though many devotees awoke to the fact that the Watchtower Society was not God's mouthpiece and departed, the society's followers had still increased. Yes, the society greatly benefited from stating that the world would end in 1975—but many Witnesses were financially and emotionally devastated by this incorrect prediction. And yet many remained faithful—so brainwashed that they could not see the truth.

Chapter Three

Behind the Walls
of the Kingdom Halls

Let us now take a look at some of the day-to-day practices that occur behind the walls of Kingdom Halls and determine if they coincide with Scripture and common sense.

The Claim of "Great Love"—True or False?

Watchtower publications continually boast of the "great love" that exists among Witnesses. "Show me another group that has so much love!" is its challenge. A four-page tract entitled "Will All People Ever Love One Another?" was widely distributed around the world in the fall of 1997, and it made this boast: "What about today? Is Christlike love practiced by anybody? The *Encyclopedia Canadiana* observes. 'The work of the Jehovah's Witnesses is the revival and the re-establishment of the primitive Christianity practiced by Jesus and his disciples. . . . All are brothers.'"

Is the Watchtower Society not patting its own back here? Proverbs 27:2 says, "Let another man praise thee, and not thine own mouth; a stranger and not thine own lips." Few outsiders who have taken a close look at the Watchtower Society and its adherents would agree that there is extraordinary love among Witnesses. In fact, this is a rather strange boast, because the society has no way of making a comparison. The leaders of the Watchtower Society have never been inside another church—at least not since 1935—so from personal experience there is no standard with which to compare itself. We can liken this to an art exhibition with only one picture on display. The artist boasts that his picture is the best in the gallery, which is *true*; but if fifty other pictures were also displayed, would his boast still be true?

Related to this is another astounding claim of the Watchtower Society found in the October 1, 1999, *Watchtower*. They state: "They [Jehovah's Witnesses] are actually the happiest group of people on earth." This is rather puzzling for several reasons. Jehovah's Witnesses are not able to attend the meetings of other religious groups, so how can they really know? Also, if the Jehovah's Witnesses are really "the happiest group of people on earth," and there is so much love among them, why do 35% of those in America eventually leave?

Many who become involved in the Watchtower have looked in vain for this kind of love. One Witness told me he did not find love in his congregation. He thought maybe it was just his congregation, since the society claims there really is love among Witnesses. He tried several other Kingdom Halls, but his search for the "great love" he was promised proved to be fruitless.

Even those who find a sense of belonging and acceptance in the Jehovah's Witnesses later discover that their so-called love is conditional. If a Witness scales down in his door-to-door visitation or attendance at the meetings, the love of his fellow worshipers begins to wane. When a person stops attending the meetings altogether, the love, if it ever was there, completely stops.

Busyness: Meetings and Door-to-Door Visitation

Should you begin studying with a Jehovah's Witness, you have no idea how busy you will become if you take the next step and are baptized into the Watchtower Society. Intense pressure is put on all Witnesses to attend five meetings every week. Add to that the travel time to the Kingdom Hall. In addition, Witnesses are required to spend a lot of time studying Watchtower material in preparation for meetings, where they will be quizzed on the material.

There is also pressure to do door-to-door visitation—in America, the expected commitment is at least ten hours every month. If you raise this subject prior to being baptized into their faith, you would be led to believe that this is optional. Not so! It is considered mandatory.

When a person becomes a Jehovah's Witness, the society takes preference over the individual's family. Studying Watchtower publications is considered more important than household chores. "Field service"—going door to door—is a higher priority than family responsibilities. If a married person becomes a Jehovah's Witness and the spouse does not, the marriage often ends in divorce, because the Jehovah's Witness partner is more dedicated to the Watchtower Society and its dictates than to maintaining a healthy marriage.

A man who had been a Jehovah's Witness for twenty years phoned me and expressed his frustration. Not only was he burdened with all the meetings and the pressure to put in ten hours a month in door-to-door visitation, but he also had to work three jobs to make a living because his wife was a Pioneer! (A Pioneer spends *ninety* hours a month in door-to-door visitation.)

One Solution for All Problems

It doesn't matter what problem a Jehovah's Witness is experiencing—marital conflict, raising children, work pressures, financial difficulties, fatigue, sickness, depression, struggling with sin—the answer is always the same: "You need to spend more time reading Watchtower publications, attending meetings and faithfully going door to door." Ironically, in many cases the root of the problem is the stress they are experiencing from the many Watchtower activities they are already required to do.

Thinking and Behaving Alike

Unity on major doctrines is certainly desirable for those who profess membership in a religious fellowship, but the Watchtower Society seeks complete uniformity among its followers—a uniformity that goes beyond doctrine into every aspect of life.

God has made all individuals different; He never ordained uniformity. Different cultures have distinctive traits, concepts and ways of living. The Watchtower Society, however, tries to make everyone the same. All Jehovah's Witnesses, worldwide, have to study, believe, practice and act alike. All worldwide branch offices (over 100) are controlled from the headquarters in Brooklyn, New York. The director of each branch is trained in Brooklyn and sent out to serve in various locales. All are males, and most are white.

There is a uniform dress code to which all Jehovah's Witnesses—children and adults—must conform. There is even one mail-order store from which Jehovah's Witnesses can order their briefcases and handbags, since they all carry the same type.

It matters not what Kingdom Hall you visit, meetings all follow the same format. They are conducted according to clearly stipulated directions. They must start exactly on time and end on time.

Jehovah's Witnesses are all expected to spend the same amount of time in door-to-door visitation. Parents of small children are expected to spend as much time on visitation as singles or childless couples. Though it takes far more hours per day to make a living in some countries than in others, it makes no difference. Jehovah's regulations must be maintained.

I have observed Jehovah's Witnesses in Japan, Korea, Romania and Portugal, as well as America, and they even *walk* alike. But I readily understand why they move so slowly as they trudge from door to door. Wouldn't you?

When it comes to religious material, the society tells its followers what they can read and what they can't. The ordinary member is not even allowed to freely read the old Watchtower publications found in Kingdom Hall archives. Permission must be obtained from an elder, and one of the elders must be present when the member examines them. Should you ask permission more than once, the elder will ask for a reason, and you are likely to be refused. The society apparently realizes that there have been some drastic changes in doctrine and practice introduced since the older books were published.

The society tells you with whom you can associate and with whom you can't. It even tells you how you ought to think, if you are allowed to think at all. An "independent thought" is often considered to be from the devil and a sin.

Children are told what they can and can't do in school. No matter what kind of physical skills the young person possesses, he or she is not allowed to participate in competitive sports. Those who have the intellectual capacity and desire for higher education are strongly discouraged from doing so.

These are just a few of the ways in which Jehovah's Witnesses must conform. No room is left for individuality or distinct cultural differences.

My upbringing taught the benefits of allowing young people the freedom to make their own individual choices, so that they can learn how to make good ones. Could this restrictive conditioning explain why many Jehovah's Witnesses do not know how to act or make proper decisions when they are outside their controlled environment? It surely makes it hard for Jehovah's Witnesses to leave the society. Many would like to leave the Watchtower fold, but it is frightening to face life as an individual after being controlled for so long.

Gloating over Those Who Depart

The Watchtower Society elders and publications continually stress their right and obligation to disfellowship apostates and immoral people. Why does this get so much press?

Those who are disfellowshiped or who voluntarily disassociate themselves from the Witnesses are given no opportunity to defend themselves or explain their circumstances for leaving. An elder will stand before the congregation and read the name of the one who has been cut off.

What goes on in the minds of those who hear this pronouncement? Since the Watchtower Society teaches that the organization is *always right* and only unrepentant sinners and apostates are disfellowshiped, and since Jehovah's Witnesses have heard this repeated so many times, the prevailing attitude is that one is either a Jehovah's Witness or a sinner.

It is true that many Jehovah's Witnesses will, on leaving the Watchtower Society, enter into a life of sin. They assume that their only alternative, now that they are no longer a Witness, is a life of drunkeness, drugs, sex, etc.

But what if a disfellowshiped Witness *does not* succumb to worldly ways? If a person leaves the society yet still lives a moral life, this proves the Watchtower wrong. So while the Watchtower Society seems to condemn sin, it is not pleased when those who leave the fellowship do not fall into a life of sin and debauchery.

Why so Busy?

The governing body of the Watchtower Society does not want their adherents to have any time to think. They realize that if people are allowed time to read the Bible, they will never become Jehovah's Witnesses; or, if already members, they will eventually leave the society. For this reason, only Watchtower publications are allowed in meetings and so-called "Bible studies." By having to attend five meetings a week and being pushed to spend ten hours a month going door to door, Jehovah's Witnesses don't have time to consider their situation. This is a form of mind control.

Chapter Four

The Inner Workings of the Society

It is sensible to ask how anyone could get involved with a group that has 100% control over its adherents' behavior, emotions, thoughts and access to information. Who would want to join a group with this coercive approach, in which disciples are kept in constant fear? By getting an inside look at the ways in which the Watchtower organization operates, we begin to get an answer to that question.

Easy to Get In, Hard to Get Out

When a person who is not already related to a Watchtower member becomes involved, it is usually because of an emotional need. Sometimes the individual has moved into the area and is lonely. The person may have suffered a major upheaval such as job loss, divorce, trouble with children, or a prolonged illness in the family. Some become involved when facing a midlife crisis or a bitter experience with a church.

At such a time as this, the Jehovah's Witnesses come along and seem to show concern for this lonely individual. And who doesn't appreciate finding a friend? Since the Jehovah's Witnesses spend so many hours going door to door, they learn what type of people make the best prospects; they are not interested in recruiting those who really know their Bibles and have stable family lives.

At the outset, the Jehovah's Witnesses seem to have biblical answers to some of life's problems—and their knowledge can appear quite impressive. (Jehovah's Witnesses actually have very little Bible knowledge, but what distorted facts they know, they know well, because instruction is repeated over and over at their meetings.)

One of the first things Witnesses teach a person is that they will encounter opposition from those who are trying to prevent them from becoming a true follower of Jehovah. They say that this opposition is from the devil, who is trying to keep him or her from "the truth." Thus, when friends or relatives try to warn a Watchtower recruit, it usually makes that person more determined than ever to continue studying with the Witnesses.

There are scores of groups, however, that claim to be "the one true religion," so it is obviously a good idea to listen to all the advice one can get. In fact, no matter what religious group one is associated with, opposition is typical. This doesn't prove the Watchtower or any other sect to be the true religion; it only proves that people who question your actions are concerned about you. They want you to consider your decision carefully and not join a group due to an emotional need.

In addition, the Watchtower Society does not want its

prospects to have contact with anyone who has left the organization. It teaches that any information from former members is "apostate" and "anti"—even if much of the material includes quotes from previously written Watchtower publications. This should make anyone suspicious.

Visiting Jehovah's Witnesses usually do not tell their prospects that they will be expected (almost forced) to attend five grueling meetings every week. (On a weekday night they have three meetings back to back: a Bible study for 25 minutes, a Theocratic Ministry School for 35 minutes, and a Service Meeting for 35 minutes. On Sunday they have two meetings: a Public Talk for 30 minutes, and a Watchtower Study for one hour.) Once a person begins attending and shows some interest, the next step is to insist on door-to-door visitation.

The Watchtower indoctrination gradually creates great fear in the sect's members. They are taught that if they do not continue in "God's organization" they will be destroyed when Armageddon occurs. If they have children, they will be told that God will kill their children at Armageddon, right before their eyes, if they do not remain faithful to and active in "Jehovah's organization."

In order to become a "good" Jehovah's Witness, one has to lock up one's mind to independent thinking. One thing the Watchtower Society can't tolerate is people who ask thought-provoking questions and want to deductively understand the group's teachings and practices. The society wants "conformity" at any cost. All must dress in the same style, carry the same kind of briefcase or pocketbook, etc. Thus Jehovah's Witnesses lose their own identity.

In a letter to me, a woman whose daughter had become

a Jehovah's Witness wrote, "After my daughter and son-in-law became Jehovah's Witnesses, they lived with us for the next five and a half months. I will spare you the details of this time except to say they did what they were expected to do and said what they were expected to say, and life was *more than* difficult. I did a lot of crying at this time (a *lot!*). This young lady *looked* like my daughter and her voice *sounded* like my daughter—*but* it really was not my daughter." (Emphasis in original letter.)

Another lady confessed that after studying with the Witnesses for a number of years, she felt that she was losing her identity. She had become hardened by her association with the society and had no compassion. Reports of this sort are common.

At first Jehovah's Witnesses will spend a great deal of time socializing with a prospect, and the congregation will seem quite hospitable. But there is a catch: Any time a Witness spends with a prospect counts toward the mandatory ten hours of "field service" each month. Once the prospect becomes a baptized Jehovah's Witness, however, social time no longer counts as field service, so these new "friendships" disappear as the veteran Witnesses spend their time with someone else— someone they can credit toward their required ten hours.

In due time the new convert discovers that he no longer has any true friends—no one in whom he can truly confide. Jehovah's Witnesses are taught to squeal and spy on each other. The elders—the ruling body in the Kingdom Hall— eventually know every move you make. So if you have any real questions or doubts about the organization and dare to breathe these to anyone, it will be brought to the attention of the elders. The worst offense possible would be to question the functioning of the society—to ask where it gets its authority, why its teachings keep changing and so on. Even for something much less serious you can find yourself standing before a "judicial committee," a group made up of three elders. You will stand there alone. Advocates for the accused are not permitted. You will be presumed guilty before you enter the room. One such reprimand is enough to make you realize that you dare not confide in anyone. You must settle for very shallow relationships.

The society has developed a clever system. From the very beginning it urges a person to break off relationships with outside friends and neighbors because "they are worldly and evil." An upright person—so the injunction goes—shouldn't want to associate with anyone who might have a bad influence on him. And this extends to near relations, if they are not amenable to Watchtower doctrine. (Jehovah's Witnesses don't take the Bible seriously when it says, "Honor your father and mother," or in its teaching that a husband and wife are to be one.)

Before long a Witness ends up having no one to associate with outside of the Watchtower Society. By the time you realize the Watchtower Society is not what it claims to be—that there is no real love, that the meetings are repetitious and dull, and that you can't question the organization but must conform to all its dictates—you no longer have any outside associations.

Thus the Watchtower Society, just like other cults, makes it difficult for anyone to leave. It will say, "Yes, we have faults and make mistakes, but where will you go if you leave this organization? Other groups have many more faults than we do." A person cannot just "walk away" from the Watchtower.

Those who dare to step out of line are judged by a judicial committee, found guilty, and—if unrepentant—disfellowshipped. After that, they are shunned: No Jehovah's Witness is allowed to speak to them, let alone have any dealings with them—not even their own flesh and blood.

Consider this case: Mrs. R.W. came to realize that the Watchtower religion was false, but her daughter, son-in-law and granddaughter are still in the organization. Were she to leave, she would never see them again, especially her granddaughter. If her granddaughter got married, she would be excluded from the wedding. For this reason, she spends the minimum time (one hour a month) going door to door, just so she can continue to see her family.

I am convinced that if the Watchtower Society were to proclaim a complete amnesty for everyone who wanted to leave—that is, discontinue its practice of shunning—a large percentage of Jehovah's Witnesses would run as quickly as they could from the organization.

It doesn't matter with what offense a Jehovah's Witness is charged, the shunning policy is the same for all. In contrast, the Bible urges us to try to restore an erring brother in love. How can this be accomplished where there is no communication and the disfellowshipped person is treated disrespectfully? If he has really committed a sin, he needs help. This policy of accusing, judging and punishing while offering no help actually entices people into sin. The expelled person reasons, "Since I am accused of being bad, I may as well start acting as bad as they say I am." And he abandons his previously held moral beliefs.

How did Jesus treat sinners? Jesus ate and associated with them. He went home with Zacchaeus, who was a tax collector and greatly despised by the Jews. Jesus went after the lost and erring sheep. Jesus clearly taught that we are to love our enemies and do good even to those who persecute us. Obviously, a true Christian will not enter into the sinful acts of the world, but he must not cut himself off from worldly people or he will never have an opportunity to tell others about the wonderful salvation found in Jesus Christ.

The present disfellowshipping policy of the Watchtower Society certainly cannot be said to be biblical. A woman who grew up as a Jehovah's Witness recently exclaimed, "How can the Watchtower Society be of God when it breaks up families and relationships?"

The Society and God—the Same or Not?

If Jehovah's Witnesses question their elders, or children ask their parents about the mistakes, false speculations and constant changes in the society's teachings and practices, they will be accused of griping and finding fault with God. They will be reminded that the society is "God's organization," so complaints about the society are really complaints against God. Jehovah's Witnesses are thereby induced to think of God and the Watchtower Society as being one and the same. This psychological sleight-of-hand heaps guilt on any Witness who seeks answers to legitimate questions.

Furthermore, when Witnesses come to realize that the Watchtower Society is *not* "the truth"—and many do—they often become bitter toward God, since they see Him in the same light as the Watchtower Society. As a result some turn their back on God.

On the one hand, anyone who complains or who delves critically beneath the surface is supposedly rebelling against

God. On the other hand, if someone provides clear evidence of mistakes in this supposedly "theocratic, God-run" organization, the society and elders are quick to respond, "Yes, we do make mistakes, and we do not claim to be infallible—because there are human, fallible men in the organization." The duplicity is obvious.

Redefining Christian Terms

One thing that makes it so difficult to understand what the Watchtower Society teaches is its practice of taking the very words Christians have used for centuries and giving them *drastically different meanings*. Those familiar with these terms might think that the Watchtower Society believes the same biblical truths Christianity has upheld since the beginning of the church. This has been done with the deliberate purpose of deceiving people. Of course, a Jehovah's Witness will not explain the society's terminology until pushed to do so, and even then will not give a complete explanation; a prospective convert must be properly brainwashed a little at a time. Only after being baptized is a person likely to find out what the Watchtower Society really believes.

Since the society uses the same vocabulary as biblical Christianity, outsiders are often deceived into thinking it is just another denomination of the Christian faith. But the Watchtower clearly teaches that *it alone* is the *only organization* that has "the truth," and that all other denominations and religions are false and controlled by the devil.

How Doctrines and Practices Are Formulated

The Watchtower Society claims to be based on the Bible,

and most of its members know very well the few verses that they assume prove its teachings. They can even quote some Greek and Hebrew words. In the final analysis, however, they use only about six percent of the Bible. This is because the society's leaders did not formulate its doctrines and practices by reading and studying the Bible, but by conceiving them on their own and then searching for verses to substantiate their views. This may seem like a strong statement, but it is corroborated by history.

When the organization's human originator, Charles Taze Russell, started his Bible class, he taught that hell was not a literal place of suffering but only "man's common grave." He borrowed this false idea from Christian Adventists and Christadelphians, two groups with whom he was associated. (It is interesting that one of Russell's main doctrines was clearly derived from the teaching of two groups which he later claimed to be apostate.)

After Russell rejected the doctrine of hell, his next step was to "water down" sin. While believing that no one is perfect and everyone makes mistakes, Russell denied that humans are basically sinful and personally responsible for their sins. It was only logical, he then reasoned, to also deny the deity of Jesus Christ. After all, if humans are such un-godly sinners, only God could possibly provide the remedy for our sins. But if humans are not really ungodly sinners, there really is no need for a divine Savior. Finally, if man is not really so sinful, according to Russell, he does not need the Holy Spirit to sanctify his life. He can improve himself through his own effort. So Russell also dispensed with the Holy Spirit.

This was nothing less than a wholesale dismantling of

biblical truth through human reasoning. In doing so, however, Russell was not espousing anything original, but was only parroting the Arian view—a heresy dating back many centuries.

Russell also claimed he was the only one who could properly interpret the Bible. As a result people were discouraged from studying the Bible on their own. The Watchtower Society produced publications that provided the "proper meaning" of Scripture. (Of course, the "proper meaning" has been modified and even reversed by the society many times over the years, but this is what happens when one relies on an interpretation of the Bible based on man's reasoning rather than relying on the Holy Spirit.)

In short, Russell formulated his own doctrines and beliefs, and then looked for Bible passages (sometimes just a part of a verse or one word from a verse) that *seemed* to prove what he had already decided. The society continues this practice, digging up three or four verses that seem to agree with its previously determined teachings and then saying that since these verses "prove" its ideas, all other verses on the subject must conform to what it already claims to have proven.

One who is familiar with the whole Bible, however, or who reads their proof-texts in context, soon realizes that the Watchtower Society is not a Bible-based religion. Here is an example: The society denies the deity of Jesus Christ and uses John 14:28b, John 20:17b and Mark 13:32 to "prove" they are right.

• John 14:28b says, "For my Father is greater than I."

• John 20:17b says, "I ascend unto my Father and your

Father; and to my God, and your God." (The argument is that if Jesus had a God, then He could not be God.)

- Mark 13:32 says, "But of that day and that hour knoweth no man, no, not the angels, which are in heaven, neither the Son, but the Father." (The society maintains that if Jesus were God He would know everything.)

By the society's reasoning, since these three verses "prove" that Jesus is not God, all other Scripture concerning the deity of Christ must be interpreted in the light of these verses. If they acknowledged that Jesus was *both* man *and* God, they would not have this problem, because they would see that these verses refer to His human nature and not His divine nature.

Jehovah's Witnesses do not investigate their own religion. To do so would be contrary to a cardinal rule of their society: All doubts arise from the devil. They gullibly, therefore, accept what they have been taught rather than thinking for themselves. If you talk with a Witness about religion for any length of time, you will realize that everything they say is a matter of rote—something they have memorized and are parroting—not a conviction that has been arrived at through reflection or independent study.

Placing Literature: A Money-Making Operation

Most people are not aware that 70% of the income of the Watchtower Society comes from profit on the literature they distribute. For many years (and this is still true in many countries), there was a stipulated price for its magazines and books. As Jehovah's Witnesses went from door to door they would tell people that they were selling the magazines and books "just for the price of printing." This is not true. The society actually made a great deal of profit from their material.

A few years ago, however, they changed their policy in the US and some other countries. To avoid paying sales taxes, the current practice is to ask for contributions. Individual Jehovah's Witnesses, however, are required to purchase the material they distribute at the full price set by the society. As they distribute this literature and receive contributions—in many cases far more than the item is worth—the society strongly suggests that the money be put in a special envelope and turned into headquarters. This way, the material is often paid for twice.

The Watchtower Society publishes at least one new book a year, which every member (not just one per family) is expected to buy ("make a contribution for"). In the English language alone, this can easily mean sales of a million copies or more. Imagine the profit in this! Press runs this large can bring printing costs down to just pennies per book. When Jehovah's Witnesses tell you that the society does not make a profit on its literature, either they do not know how the corporation operates (which is not surprising, since the Watchtower never distributes financial statements), or they are not telling the truth.

All Non-Watchtower Literature Is Forbidden

The Watchtower Society is based on the latest teachings, which are found in their publications. Witnesses regularly go from door to door, urging people to read the society's literature, but they themselves absolutely refuse to read any other religious literature, no matter where it comes from. They won't even read outdated Watchtower material.

The society claims that other literature is "religious pornography," which would be harmful for followers to read. This sort of reasoning is similar to the method used by the Communists. They too controlled the type of literature people could read; this rule kept their citizens under its power.

If the Watchtower Society really taught "the truth" from the Bible, then it would be teaching its followers how to properly discern between truth and error. Those who have the truth are able to let people read both sides of the story. But the Watchtower Society will not let its people be exposed to other views of the Bible, because if it did its followers would begin to think for themselves and see the errors of the Watchtower way.

"New Light"—Where From?

When confronted with the fact that the Watchtower Society has made many false interpretations of prophetic scriptures, has formerly practiced many things that it now considers "pagan," and has changed many of its teachings, the Witnesses are taught to respond by saying, "Yes, we have made mistakes, but we are willing to admit our mistakes. But you must realize that we are making progress, and God is continually giving us 'new light' so we have had to adjust some [actually, just about all] of our teachings and practices."

The society's publications continually quote Proverbs 4:18, which in its *New World Translation* says, "But the path of the righteous ones is like the bright light that is getting lighter and lighter until the day is firmly established." This is just a polite way of making God responsible for all their mistakes.

Charles Russell made one true statement that every Jehovah's Witness should read and take to heart. It was published in the February 1881 issue of *Zion's Watch Tower* magazine (now entitled *The Watchtower*).

> If we were following a man, undoubtedly it would be different with us; undoubtedly one human idea would contradict another and that which was light one or two or six years ago would be regarded as darkness now. But with God there is no variableness, neither shadow of turning, and so it is with *truth*; any knowledge or light coming from God must be like its author. A new view of truth never can contradict a former truth. *"New light"* never extinguishes older *"light,"* but adds to it. If you were lighting up a building containing seven gas jets you would not extinguish one every time you lit another, but would add one light to another and they would be in harmony and thus give increase of light. So it is with the light of truth; the true increase is by adding to, not by substituting one for another.

In contrast to Russell's statement, every time the Watchtower Society comes up with some "new light," it has to extinguish a previous "new light." For instance, prior to 1931 it was acceptable for Jehovah's Witnesses to receive vaccinations, but on February 4, 1931, vaccinations were forbidden and claimed to be "a direct violation of the law of Jehovah God." However, they changed their mind again, and on April 15, 1952, they once again allowed Jehovah's Witnesses to be vaccinated.

From the beginning of the Watchtower Society in 1874 until 1929, the leaders taught that the "superior authorities" mentioned in Romans 13:1 meant "the government rulers of this world." But in 1929 Joseph Rutherford (then the leader of the society) changed it to mean "Jehovah God and His Son in heaven." The previous view was declared to be a view of the devil, and anyone who held to that view was being led by the devil. But strangely, in 1963, it was changed back to mean "the government rulers of this world"—the very same view which previously was supposed to have been inspired by the devil!

The society supposedly received some more "new light" in 1967. Before then organ transplants were allowed, but in that year's November 15 issue of *Watchtower,* the society reversed itself and emphatically declared,

> When men and science conclude that this normal process will no longer work and they suggest removing the organ and replacing it directly with an organ from another human, this is simply a short-cut. Those who submit to such operations are thus living off the flesh of another human. *That is cannibalistic.* However, in allowing man to eat animal flesh, Jehovah God did not grant permission for humans to try to perpetuate their lives by *cannibalistically* taking into their bodies human flesh, whether chewed or in the form of whole organs or body parts taken from others [emphasis added].

But this "new light" turned out to be false, because in the March 15, 1980, *Watchtower*, the society once again reversed itself and said that organ transplants were not considered cannibalistic. Each individual was now allowed to decide for himself. Wonderful! But what about the many Jehovah's Witnesses who died during this thirteen-year period because the Watchtower Society said an organ transplant was cannibalistic and forbidden by God?

Many, many more examples could be offered, but these are sufficient to show that the so-called "new light" of the Watchtower Society is not necessarily "true light." However, when this "new light" is received, it is not presented as being the ideas or theories of the men who constitute the governing body of the Watchtower Society. It is promulgated as coming from God.

Even though the Society has made so many mistakes in the past and has taught doctrine that is false and now declared pagan, a Jehovah's Witness is *not free to determine if he wants to accept the "new light" or not.* He is compelled to change his views to conform to the Watchtower's new teachings. Even if he is convinced that the Watchtower is wrong, he must present the Watchtower's "new light" as being true. If he doesn't, he will be disfellowshipped.

This is a very serious issue. This false "new light" presented by the Watchtower Society has hurt many people. What about those who contracted smallpox because they submitted to the Watchtower teaching and refused to be vaccinated? What about those who went blind because they refused a cornea transplant during the years 1967 to 1980? It has been estimated that up to three thousand people were disfellowshipped for not going along with Rutherford's "new light" on Romans 13:1.

What about those who believed the "new light" that the world would end in October 1975 and sold their homes, sometimes their businesses, or only worked part time in order to go door to door? Not only did they suffer tremendous financial loss, but also great humiliation when the Watchtower told them in 1976 that they were "just over-zealous" and were foolish for doing such things. The Watchtower may be getting "new light," but it certainly is not the "true light."

Moreover, if the Watchtower Society is consistent with its own publications, it can no longer use the feeble excuse of "new light" to cover up its many mistakes. Keeping in mind the concept of "new light" as derived from Proverbs

4:18 (that the light will get brighter and brighter "until the day is firmly established"), look at the following statement from the July 15, 1996, *Watchtower*:

> After many years in God's service, one brother wrote: "I am so thankful that I have lived in the knowledge of Jehovah's purposes from these early days just prior to 1914 when all was not so clear . . . to this day when the truth shines like the noonday sun."

Let us compare this statement (published without a hint of disagreement) to the Watchtower's interpretation of Proverbs 4:18. In 1914 the "sun" (the truth found in the teachings of Charles Russell) was just beginning to rise like the "first gleam of dawn"—not very clear. Down through the years the light has supposedly been getting brighter and brighter. But the Watchtower Society now claims that we are in the "last days," and the light is like the "noonday sun." If this is really true, then the Watchtower Society can't continue to get any *more* "new light" because its teachings are already like the noonday sun—as bright as they can possibly be!

Others Preach the Kingdom Too

Most Jehovah's Witnesses take great pride in the false assumption that they are the only ones who are "preaching the good news of the Kingdom of God." In an article published in the March 1, 1993, *Watchtower*, people were warned to prepare for the end times. They were also encouraged to seek those heeding the global sign of the last days. It went on to say, "These are easily identifiable, for they alone are obeying Jesus' command to preach the good news of the Kingdom worldwide." The Society feels this claim is one of the proofs that it is truly "Jehovah's Organization."

This claim of the Watchtower is not based on any kind of firm foundation. Even a very shallow investigation would reveal that many religious groups that use the Bible preach a literal kingdom in which Jesus Christ will rule over this earth in righteousness for one thousand years. The true church of Jesus Christ, made up of millions of born-again Christians, has gone into all the world with the message of the "Kingdom," so the Watchtower's claim is not based upon accurate knowledge.

It is interesting to note in the Bible the connection between the preaching of the kingdom and the proclaiming of Jesus:

- Acts 8:12 says, "But when they believed Philip preaching the things concerning the kingdom of God, and the name of Jesus Christ, they were baptized, both men and women."

- Acts 28:23 reads, "To whom he expounded and testified the kingdom of God, persuading them concerning Jesus, both out of the law of Moses and out of the prophets."

- Acts 28:31 states, "Preaching the kingdom of God, and teaching those things which concern the Lord Jesus Christ."

Jehovah's Witnesses continually keep talking about "Jehovah" but not much about "Jesus." Why does the Watchtower Society place so much emphasis on the kingdom and not on Jesus? Something doesn't add up!

Chapter Five

Mistakes Made by the Society

Every Kingdom Hall has a sizable library of old Watchtower publications, but these are rarely used. The society informs its elders not to allow these books and magazines to be taken from the hall, and they discourage people from reading them. Why? Because anyone who looked into these out-of-date writings would realize very quickly that the Watchtower Society is not based on the unchanging Word of God; the organization's teachings and practices keep changing over the years.

Most Jehovah's Witnesses are unwilling to look at the society's old publications even if someone offers them copies to read. They will say, "I have no interest in that old stuff." Yet when the this material first came out, it was proclaimed as "new light," the "truth of God" set forth by the "faithful and discreet slave," and had to be believed—no questions asked. Indeed, some of what is taught today will be considered "old stuff" in just a few years.

Jehovah's Witnesses who have been in the organization for any length of time once believed and taught the very things the society now considers "old stuff." It has been declared to be a wrong interpretation of prophecy, a false precept or something now classified as "pagan." If the society's historical trends of the past century are any indication, much of what is being taught *today* will be considered false, pagan and outdated in just a few short years. In short, the Watchtower Society can never point to a time in its history when it has taught "all truth"—because anything that can change is *not* "the truth."

The Society's Mistakes Are Costly

When Jehovah's Witnesses are presented with proof that their leaders have made mistakes (of which there are many), their pat answer is, "We don't claim to be inspired, and our leaders are only human, fallible men." They feel that this confession takes care of the problem. Then they will usually add, "At least, when we make a mistake, we admit it."

The only problem is the Watchtower Society never admits that it has made a mistake. It simply comes out with some new teaching (often just the opposite of what it has taught in the past) and says it is making an "adjustment" or "fine-tuning" or presenting "a clearer understanding" on the subject. While the society has admitted that it has speculated a few times, especially in setting dates for the end of this present world system, it passes off its errors by saying it was a little "over-zealous" to see God's kingdom established on earth.

But these errors have been very costly for many Witnesses, and the society never makes any kind of restitution for the losses its many mistakes have caused. For example, a number of people sold their homes and went into full-time pioneering a few years before the various times the Watchtower said the world would end (1914, 1925, the early 1940s, 1975, 1994 and before the end of the twentieth century).

Of particular note is the 1975 date. Even though many Watchtower articles as far back as 1967 stated that the world would end in October 1975, the Watchtower Society had the audacity to print in its July 15, 1976, *Watchtower* that it did *not* prophesy or speculate about a 1975 date for the end of the world. Rather, the 1976 article explained, some over-zealous Witnesses just misunderstood what was written, so it was their own fault if they sold their homes and ended up broke. It was immaterial to the society not only that this had happened, but that some of these people were older and could not easily start over. The article said:

> It may be that some who have been serving God have planned their lives according to a mistaken view of just what was to happen on a certain date [October 1975] or in a certain year. They may have, for this reason, put off or neglected things that they otherwise would have cared for. But they have missed the point of the Bible's warning concerning the end of this system of things, thinking that Bible chronology reveals the specific date. . . .

> Did Jesus mean that we should adjust our financial and secular affairs so that our resources would just carry us to a certain date that we might think marks the end? . . . "Well, we'll put it off because the time is so near for this system of things to go"?

> However, say that you are one who counted heavily on a date, and, commendably, set your attention more strictly on the urgency of the times and the need of the people to hear. And say you now, temporarily, feel somewhat disappointed: are you really the loser? Are you really hurt? We believe you can say that you have gained and profited by taking this conscientious course. Also, you have been enabled to get a really mature, more reasonable viewpoint.

Now let us look at what was printed in the Watchtower Society's monthly brochure *Kingdom Ministry,* May 1974.

> Yes, the end of this system is so very near! Is that not reason to increase our activity? . . . Reports are heard of brothers selling their homes and property and planning to finish out the rest of their days in this old system in the pioneer service. Certainly this is a fine way to spend the short time remaining before the wicked world's end.—1 John 2:17

It was not until five years later that the society finally mentioned, in their March 15, 1980 *Watchtower,* that it *might* have written some things suggesting that Armageddon would occur in October 1975.

The forbidding of blood transfusions is another very costly false teaching. The society made receiving blood a disfellowshipping offense in 1961. As a result (by a very conservative estimate), at least 200,000 Witnesses needlessly died, many of them children. Then in 1999 the Watchtower Society *drastically changed* its stand on blood transfusions. When the edict first appeared, all blood was forbidden. Now, however, certain parts of human blood may be accepted: albumin, immune globulins, Factor VIII, Factor IX and circulating blood. (The parts that must still be refused are plasma, red cells, white cells, platelets and stored blood.) What a senseless loss of life due to a perspective that the Watchtower leaders are still not clear about.

In addition, the society's opposition to military service has caused a great deal of suffering. The November 1, 1939 *Watchtower* defended "neutrality" and said that it was wrong for Witnesses to go into the military or even accept civilian service in place of the draft, which some countries allow. During World War II and the Vietnam War, many Jehovah's

Witnesses went to jail. Naturally they suffered in jail, as did their families, and many could not obtain employment after their release due to their prison record.

A case involving civilian service in the Netherlands and what the society declared at that time is found in the December 8, 1974, *Awake*.

> But Jehovah's witnesses in the Netherlands have refused, not only military service, but also any noncombatant work offered as a substitute. The Scriptural reason for their stand will be considered later in this article. . . .
>
> One of the first points of discussion presented by the forum was this: "That you wish no part in performing military service is clear and needs no further explanation. But what really is your objection to civil, alternative service?"
>
> The Witnesses explained that it is not that they are opposed to civil service as such, but, rather, it is a matter of strict neutrality. Therefore, any work that is merely a substitute for military service would be unacceptable to Jehovah's witnesses.
>
> Other questions narrowed the issue down still further. "When a person objects to military service," the government's agents declared, "he passes from military jurisdiction on to civil jurisdiction and from that moment has nothing at all to do with the military. Why, then, is the accepting of such civil service still so objectionable?"
>
> Willingly accepting such work is objectionable to the Christian because of what God's law says about the matter: "You were bought with a price, stop becoming slaves of men." (1 Cor. 7:23) Civilian servitude as a substitute from military service would be just as objectionable to the Christian. In effect, he would thereby become a part of the world instead of keeping separate as Jesus commanded.

In the September 22, 1966, *Awake*, there was a similar

incident in Sweden where the Jehovah's Witnesses refused to accept any substitute for military service.

But something happened in 1996, and the Watchtower Society decided that the Bible no longer forbade Jehovah's Witnesses from accepting civilian service in place of being drafted into the military. The May 1, 1996, *Watchtower* states under the heading "Civilian Service":

> However, there are lands where the State, while not allowing exemption for ministers of religion, nevertheless acknowledges that some individuals may object to military service. Many of these lands make provision for such conscientious individuals not to be forced into military service. In some places a required civilian service, such as useful work in the community, is regarded as nonmilitary national service. Could a dedicated Christian undertake such service? Here again, a dedicated, baptized Christian would have to make his own decision on the basis of his Bible-trained conscience.

The article goes on to say, "This has usually resulted in an excellent witness and has sometimes silenced those who falsely accused the Witnesses of being antigovernment."

It is obvious that the Watchtower Society accepts none of the responsibility for the suffering that the Witnesses have received because of *its* mistaken interpretation of the Bible. In the August 15, 1998, *Watchtower* we read:

Feeling of Having Suffered Needlessly

> In the past, some Witnesses have suffered for refusing to share in any activity that their conscience now might permit. For example, this might have been their choice years ago as to certain types of civilian service. A brother might now feel that he could conscientiously perform such without overstepping his Christian neutrality regarding the present system of things. . . .

In modern times, there have been some Witnesses who were very strict in their view of what they would or would not do. For that reason they suffered more than others. Later, increased knowledge helped them to expand their view of matters. But they have no reason to regret having earlier acted in harmony with their conscience, even when this possibly brought extra suffering. It truly is commendable that they demonstrated their willingness to suffer in faithfulness to Jehovah, to "do all things for the sake of the good news." Jehovah blesses that kind of godly devotion.

The article suggests it was the "individual's conscience," but the conscience of a Jehovah's Witness *must* coincide with what is dictated by the Watchtower Society or else he will be disfellowshipped.

Despite its vacillations, the society still claims that it is "theocratic" (ruled by God). In testimony told by George Couch in the August 1, 1998, *Watchtower*, we find the following statement: "As I look back over my lifetime in Jehovah's service, I can see that Jehovah is the one who is running this organization—not man. We are just his servants. As such, we must always look to him for direction. Once he lays out what we are to do, we should just jump in and do it together."

The society is apparently in agreement with this statement or it would not have printed it. If the society is truly ruled by God and is following His orders, then there should be *no* mistakes because God *cannot* make a mistake. A Witness contradicts himself by saying the society is "theocratic" and at the same time admits "it does make mistakes." The only honest conclusion is that the men on the governing body are disregarding the orders and directions from God and replacing them with their own. Could this explain why the society makes so many mistakes?

When individual Jehovah's Witnesses admit to others that the society makes mistakes, they often add, "The Watchtower Society makes less mistakes than other groups." But what is this supposed to mean? A religious group that admits its mistakes is not any closer to embracing *the truth* than the next group. When I am looking for a doctor, I do not want to go to the one who makes the *least* mistakes. I want one who is known for *not making mistakes*!

Motorboat Versus Sailboat

When presented with proof concerning the many and constant changes in the Watchtower Society's teachings over the years, Jehovah's Witnesses will repeat what is written in the December 1, 1981, *Watchtower* magazine. There is a picture of a sailboat with the caption "Tacking into the wind" and then next to it is written:

> However, it may have seemed to some as though that path has not always gone straightforward. At times explanations given by Jehovah's visible organization have shown adjustments, seemingly to previous points of view. But this has not actually been the case. This might be compared to what is known in navigational circles as "tacking." By maneuvering the sails the sailors can cause a ship to go from right to left, back and forth, but all the time making progress toward their destination in spite of contrary winds.

In bygone days when there were only sailboats, that might have been an acceptable explanation, but in these modern days, why take so much time in a sailboat, tacking all the time, when there are powerful motorboats that can go straight toward the desired port without all the tacking?

I do not see how the Watchtower Society can claim they are making "progress" after years of "tacking into the wind," because they come right back to the same port they left! They uphold one doctrine for years, then change to another, which is often a contradiction of the first. They then declare the earlier teaching to be pagan and false. However, they later abandon the new teaching—now considering it "pagan and false"—and go back to the original teaching.

As was mentioned before:

- From its beginning until 1929, the society taught that the "superior authorities" in Romans 13:1 were earthly governments. But in 1929 Rutherford changed this to mean "Jehovah God and Christ in heaven." However, in 1962, the society returned to the original interpretation.

- Until 1931 vaccinations were permitted. But in that year the society claimed they were forbidden according to the Bible. But somehow in 1952, the same Bible now allowed them.

- Up until 1967 organ transplants were permitted. But in 1967 they became forbidden. However, in 1980, after thirteen years of "tacking in the wind," the society's sailboat returned to the original port and once again said that organ transplants were permissible.

How can this be considered "progress"?

The Society's Attempted Compromise with Hitler

The Watchtower Society has written a great deal about the persecution that Jehovah's Witnesses received under Hitler's regime in Germany, but it fails to tell the public that it was one of the first religious groups to try to compromise with Hitler in 1933.

In the August 15, 1997, *Watchtower*, there is an article titled "They Stood Firm amid Nazi Persecution." Part of the article reads as follows:

> The fearless integrity of Jehovah's Witnesses in Nazi Germany stands out in stark contrast to the position taken by churches of Christendom. This is noted by professor of history John Weiss in his book *Ideology of Death*. He writes:
>
> "In 1934 the Evangelical church insisted the Nazis must be 'welcomed by Lutheranism,' and thanked 'the Lord God' for giving the Germans a 'pious and trusty overlord.'. . . A Protestant bishop wrote to his clergy, '[Hitler] has been sent to us by God. . . .'"
>
> But what about Jehovah's Witnesses? Professor Weiss points out that "as a group, only the Jehovah's Witnesses resisted the Nazis. . . . [They] were the ones who stood up first against the rage of the Nazi demon and who dared to make opposition according to their faith.

Now let us look at the *facts* as printed in the Watchtower Society's *1934 Yearbook*. Note that the above quotes by Protestant leaders were said to have been made in 1934 and that Jehovah's Witnesses supposedly "were the ones who stood up first" against Hitler. Let me quote from the Magdeburg Declaration, written by Joseph Rutherford, the second president of the Watchtower Society and approved by an assembly of Jehovah's Witnesses in Berlin on June 25, 1933. It was later sent to Hitler. Read carefully the quotes in this declaration and see if the Watchtower Society really did oppose Hitler.

> The present government of Germany has declared emphatically against [*sic*] Big Business oppressors and in opposition to the wrongful religious influence in the political affairs of the nation. Such is exactly our position.
>
> Instead of being against the principles advocated by the government of Germany, we stand squarely for such principles, and point

out that Jehovah God through Christ Jesus will bring about the full realization of these principles and will give the people peace and prosperity and the greatest desire of every honest heart.

A careful examination of our books and literature will disclose the fact that the very high ideals held and promulgated by the present national government are set forth in and endorsed and strongly emphasized in our publications, and show that Jehovah God will see to it that these high ideals in due time will be attained by all peoples who love righteousness and who obey the Most High. Instead, therefore, of our literature and our works being a menace to the principles of the present government we are the strongest supporters of such high ideals.

Now because it appears that Germany may soon be free from oppression and that the people may be lifted up, Satan, the great enemy, puts forth his endeavors to destroy that benevolent work in this land.

Let us remind the government and the people of Germany that it was the League of Nations compact that laid upon the shoulders of the German people the great unjust and unbearable burdens. That League of Nations compact was not brought forth by the friends of Germany.

In all these years of our work, and in the wide distribution of our books and literature, not one instance can be truthfully cited wherein our work or literature has been a menace to the government or has in any wise endangered the peace and safety of the nation.

The actual text in German is even more blatantly compromising than the English translation. This fact was recognized also in the Watchtower Society's *1974 Yearbook*, where on page 111 we read, "Many in attendance [in Berlin on June 25, 1933] were disappointed in the 'declaration,' since in many points it failed to be as strong as the brothers had hoped."

In light of the above quotes from Rutherford's Madgeburg Declaration, I will let you be the judge as to whether the Watchtower Society really stood against Hitler in his early days of power! Also note that these kind remarks made by the Watchtower Society about Hitler's Nazi Germany were made in 1933, while according to the article in the August 15, 1997 *Watchtower* the statements made by Christian leaders mentioned there were made in 1934. So, who really set the pattern for kind words and an attempt to compromise with the Hitler regime?

The shocking attempt of the Watchtower Society to compromise in this situation can be further seen in an eyewitness account by Konrad Franke, a faithful German Witness. (Konrad Franke died a faithful Witness, as shown from an article written about him in the November 1, 1983, *Watchtower* on page 31.) In Konrad Franke's account he wrote:

> I had the privilege of traveling with Brother Albert Wondres from Wiesbaden to Berlin. . . . But we were shocked when we arrived at the Tennis Hall [where the convention was held to vote on the declaration] the next morning. . . . When we entered, we found the Hall bedecked with Swastika Flags!

> . . . When the meeting started, it was preluded by a song which we had not sung for years . . . the notes were [taken from] the melody of 'Deutchland, Deutchland, uber alles'! These notes were the melody from the German National anthem!

But in spite of the clear evidence taken from a Watchtower publication that Rutherford *did* try to compromise with Hitler in 1933, the Watchtower Society had the audacity to write in the October 22, 1994, *Awake*, "We Did Not Support Hitler's War."

Heaven Was Formerly for All Jehovah's Witnesses

The Watchtower Society's teaching down through its history as to who goes to heaven, and what their role in heaven will be, is very confusing. The society *now* teaches that *only* 144,000 spirits, which are known as "the little flock" or "the bride of Christ," go to heaven to live and reign with Michael for a thousand years and that the "great crowd" can only go onto the new earth. But this has not always been so.

Charles Russell borrowed from other Adventists the teaching that only 144,000 made up the "bride of Christ" and would reign with Michael. However, Russell uniquely claimed that on October 3, 1881, this number of 144,000 was filled. (See *Zion's Watch Tower*, October and November 1881, page 289.) Yet even though new converts would only be called "the great crowd" and could not reach the same zeal and fervor as "the bride of Christ," they would still *go to heaven* and be guests of the bride. Russell taught that the "new earth" during the Millennium was for the Jewish people, which was the teaching among most Christians in Russell's day.

But in 1935 Joseph Rutherford came along with "new" insight. He contradicted Russell and said that the number of 144,000 had not been completed by October 3, 1881, but in 1935. At this time he divided the Jehovah's Witnesses into two groups, a very elite group of 144,000 who would go to heaven and reign with Michael a thousand years, and an inferior group, "the great crowd," who, he decided, were now denied entrance into heaven. These people were relegated to the new earth, where they would have to spend a thousand years rebuilding it by manual labor after the awful destruction of Armageddon. This, of course, meant that the Jewish nation would no longer be on the earth during the Millennium and not have any place in God's economy. (Note that when Rutherford made this declaration in 1935, he did not give up *his place* among "the little flock" headed for heaven. He did not offer to go to the new earth and help rebuild it.)

What right does the Watchtower Society have to say who will go to heaven and who are excluded? Jesus said in John 14:1–3 (in the words of the Watchtower Society's own translation), "Do not let your hearts be troubled. Exercise faith in God, exercise faith also in me. In the house of my Father there are many abodes. Otherwise, I would have told you, because I am going my way to prepare a place for you. Also, if I go my way and prepare a place for you, I am coming again and will receive you home to myself, that where I am you also may be."

Shouldn't All Be Born Again?

While the Watchtower Society claims that its teachings are based on the Bible and the men on the governing body are anointed with God's Spirit—which is supposed to enable them to interpret the Bible correctly—there are some basic truths that these men completely overlook or choose to ignore.

One of them is in John 3:3, where we read: "In answer Jesus said to him: 'Most truly I say to you, Unless anyone is born again, he cannot see the kingdom of God'" (NWT). Note carefully that Jesus did not use the words "kingdom of heaven," as He did in Matthew 5:3, 10 and elsewhere, but "the kingdom of God." So Jesus did not say that everyone must be born again in order to get into the "kingdom of heaven," as the Watchtower Society teaches, but that all must be born again who enter the kingdom of God.

Since Jehovah's Witnesses are still preaching the "kingdom" today, that "kingdom" has to apply to the new earth, because the society states that the "heavenly class" was completed in 1935. But the society says that only the "anointed" (the "144,000") are born again. Jesus said that everyone related to God's rule must be born again. So why is the teaching of the Watchtower Society in direct conflict with the very plain words of Jesus?

Another important verse on this subject is First John 5:1, which reads, "Everyone believing that Jesus is the Christ has been born from God" (NWT). Since the Watchtower Society teaches that those who are part of the "great crowd" are *not* born again, isn't it saying then that the "great crowd" really does not believe that Jesus is the Christ, the anointed Messiah?

But there is a more serious indictment found in Romans 8. The Watchtower Society clearly teaches that only those of the "anointed class" have God's Spirit. Every year at the Memorial observance (communion), Romans 8:16 is read to show who can partake of the elements and who can't. This verse reads: "The spirit itself bears witness with our spirit that we are God's children" (NWT). Since only those of the "anointed class" partake of the elements, then the plain conclusion is that those of the "great crowd" do not possess God's Spirit.

But what happens when we look at Romans 8:9? It states, "However, you are in harmony not with the flesh, but with the spirit, if God's spirit truly dwells in you. But if anyone does not have Christ's spirit, this one does not belong to him" (NWT). Thus, the Bible says that those who are not one of the "anointed" and do not have God's Spirit do not belong to Christ or God. In other words, they are strangers to the kingdom of God.

Romans 8:8 explains the spiritual condition of those who do not have God's Spirit. "So those who are in harmony with the flesh cannot please God" (NWT). The Bible says that only those who have God's Spirit can do what is pleasing to Him. Those who do not have God's Spirit are still in the flesh—in the old sinful nature—and they "cannot please God."

If "Theocratic," Why Mistakes?

The Watchtower Society claims that it is "theocratic," which means "run by God." If this were really true, then God would have to take responsibility for all the mistakes which the organization has made and continues to make. Anyone knows that it is impossible to accuse the all-knowing God of the Bible of continually making mistakes and changing His mind. So to grapple with this dilemma, the society says, when confronted with its many mistakes, "Of course we make mistakes. You see, we have human, sinful men on our governing body. But even the disciples had mistaken ideas and made mistakes."

First, let's discuss their excuse that "even the disciples made mistakes." Yes, the disciples did make mistakes, but they did not *teach* mistakes in the name of God and force people to believe them under the threat of being disfellowshipped. But when the apostle Peter made mistakes, the apostle Paul took action. When Peter withdrew from the

Gentiles when "certain men came from James" (Gal. 2:11–14), Paul stood up to him, because Peter was to blame.

In another instance, when those of Jerusalem (considered by the Watchtower Society to be the "governing body" of the early church) were preaching error—that the Gentiles had to be circumcised in order to be saved—Paul and others went up to Jerusalem and rebuked the governing body, and these men admitted their error.

I have never heard of any elders or any other group among the Jehovah's Witnesses going up to Brooklyn, New York, and rebuking the governing body for their errors and the governing body then admitting they had made a mistake.

Second, let's consider their statement, "We have human, sinful men on our governing body." If God is really running the organization, then the men on the governing body should only be taking orders from God and doing exactly what He instructs. Thus, if the governing body of the Watchtower Society really gets instructions from God, either it can't make any mistakes, or else they don't like the orders they receive from God and change them to suit themselves. Would this not be disobedience and insubordination?

Why would God continue to let the Watchtower Society be His "sole channel of communication to this world" when it has speculated incorrectly and made so many mistakes, especially when many of these mistakes have caused both physical and emotional suffering?

Thus, if the Watchtower Society really is "theocratic," it can't make mistakes. But since it has and continues to make mistakes, it is not "theocratic."

Jehovah's Witnesses a Cult?

In America alone there are over one thousand cults. None of them, however, admits to being a cult. But just because a group *denies* it is a cult, does not mean it is *not* a cult.

Apparently the Watchtower Society is aware that there are many people who consider them a cult. For this reason the feature article in the February 15, 1994, *Watchtower* was "Jehovah's Witnesses a Cult or Ministers of God?" The article offers the Watchtower Society's definition of a cult and explains that it is not a cult, but rather true "ministers of God." But if it is not a cult now, it *used to* be one, as defined by this article.

Watchtower publications clearly claim that God has been using their organization since 1874 when Charles Russell founded it. The 1988 Watchtower book *REVELATION: Its Grand Climax at Hand!* says, "Charles Taze Russell . . . set an outstanding example of storing up spiritual treasures in heaven." Then it quotes Hebrews 13:7, which says, "Remember them which have the rule over you, who have spoken unto you the word of God." This obviously means Charles Russell.

The February 15, 1994, *Watchtower* article identifies a cult as one "whose members derive their identity and purpose from a single, charismatic individual." This describes the early situation in the movement *exactly*. Charles Russell certainly was "a charismatic individual." He was the sole author of all the *Watchtower* articles, and he had complete rule over the movement. Actually, the early Jehovah's Witnesses were known as "Russellites," even though the present-day Watchtower Society denies it. (There were a number of groups that for various reasons broke off but continued to call themselves "Russellites" or "Bible Students." So in order to distinguish his followers from these splinter groups, Joseph Rutherford chose the name "Jehovah's Witnesses.") Also, Charles Russell was held so highly by his followers that it amounted to "creature worship." Let me give you a few quotes from Watchtower publications to prove this.

> The insistence that Russell had been "that servant" led many to regard Russell in what amounted actually to creature worship. (*Jehovah's Witnesses in the Divine Purpose*, 1959, p. 69)

> With the passing of time, however, the idea adopted by many was that C.T. Russell himself was the "faithful and wise servant." This led some into the snare of creature worship. (*1975 Yearbook of Jehovah's Witnesses*, p. 88)

> This view was prominently featured in the book published in July of 1917 by People's Pulpit Association of Brooklyn, New York. This book was called *The Finished Mystery* and furnished a commentary of the Bible books of Revelation and Ezekiel and The Song of Solomon. On its Publisher's page the book was called the "Posthumous Work of Pastor Russell." Such a book and religious attitude tended to establish a religious sect centered around a man. (*God's Kingdom of a Thousand Years Has Approached*, 1973, p. 347)

> Not strange, then, that at the beginning of this "the Lord's day" there was a tendency to establish a religious sect among those today known as the Christian witnesses of Jehovah. Charles Taze Russell, the president of the Watch Tower Bible . . . Tract Society from 1884 to 1916, did not try to set up a religious sect among the members of the Society and members of the related organization, International Bible Students Association. . . . Nevertheless, after his death on October 31, 1916, in the midst of World War I, there was a tendency to form a religious sect around his teachings and organization structure, although it was not intended to do so." (*Then Is Finished the Mystery of God*, 1969, p. 110)

Thus, the Watchtower publications clearly acknowledge that at one time the Watchtower Society was a cult since its members "derived their identity and purpose from a single, charismatic individual," Charles Russell.

But not all of this is in the past. There is an article in the March 15, 1996, *Watchtower* titled, "Behold the Loyal!" The article begins by saying,

> JOSEPH F. RUTHERFORD, who succeeded C.T. Russell as president of the Watch Tower Society in 1917, began his remarks at Russell's memorial service by saying: 'Charles Taze Russell was loyal to God, loyal to Christ Jesus, loyal to the cause of Messiah's kingdom. He was loyal to the core—yea, loyal even unto death.' Truly, that was a fine tribute to make to a faithful servant of Jehovah God. No greater tribute could we pay to any individual than to say that he met the challenge of loyalty, that he was loyal—loyal to the core.

(Remember, these remarks were made about the one who encouraged so many practices that are considered "pagan" today.) Then on page 11 there is a large picture of Charles Taze Russell. On page 12 there is a same-sized picture of Jesus Christ with the caption "Jesus truly was Jehovah's 'loyal one.'" On page 13 is a same-sized picture of Job with the caption "Job, though imperfect, proved loyal to God." Then on page 14 there is another same-sized picture of the great apostle Paul with the caption "Paul set a fine example of loyalty to Jehovah." The implication of this article is quite obvious. The Watchtower Society is *still* placing Charles Russell in the rank of Jesus Christ, Job and the apostle Paul.

Another sign of a cult mentioned in the February 15, 1994, *Watchtower* article is, "Often these leaders boast of having been divinely chosen or even of being themselves divine in nature." Charles Russell did claim that he was divinely chosen.

> The special messenger of the last Age of the Church was Charles T. Russell, born February 16, 1852. He has privately admitted his belief that he was chosen for his great work before his birth. (*The Finished Mystery*, 1917, p. 53)

> Our reason was, we have FAITH that the Lord has returned, and HE is the CHIEF REAPER in this "Harvest," that HE has been supervising the work, for now about thirty-seven years, and that HE has placed Pastor Russell in charge of the work this side of the veil. We are glad therefore to recognize him as "that servant," spoken of by the Lord; glad to recognize that the work he is doing is the work the Lord has appointed him to do, and we are glad to cooperate with him and be associated with him as much as possible. [This quote is taken from the foreword of the 1911 convention report. Emphasis is in the article.]

So we see that Charles Russell did "boast of having been divinely chosen"—which is a sign of a cult leader.

At the beginning of this February 15, 1994, article, it mentions the "Branch Davidians" in Waco, Texas. It is obvious that the *Watchtower* article regards the "Branch Dividians" to be a cult. Yet this group came out of the Adventists, the very same group that Charles Russell borrowed so many of his main teachings from—doctrines still held by the Watchtower Society today.

The article continues by describing a cult "as a small fringe religious group." When Charles Russell began the International Bible Student Association it was just "a small fringe religious group." So the Watchtower Society itself had this mark of a cult at least in the early days of the movement. However, all groups are small when they first begin. But even small cult groups can grow to become large groups—even larger than the Watchtower Society. The Watchtower Society would classify the Seventh-Day Adventists as a cult, yet the Seventh-Day Adventists have a larger active membership than the Watchtower Society. The Watchtower Society also classifies the Mormons as a cult, but the Mormons have a much larger following than the Watchtower Society and are growing at a faster rate.

So we see that defining a cult "as a small fringe religious group" is not a completely accurate definition.

Another definition in the *Watchtower* article is that "Cult members often isolate themselves from friends, family, and even society in general." Then it asks, "Is that the case with Jehovah's Witnesses?" Let us examine some of the Watchtower Society's practices and see what kind of an answer we come up with.

The Watchtower Society urges all its members to separate from their friends because they are all considered "worldly" (no matter what kind of moral character they have). Even when a person is just studying with a Jehovah's Witness, he is urged to make this break. For this reason very few Jehovah's Witnesses have close personal contact with anyone outside of the organization.

One very subtle way the society isolates its members from their family members is by not permitting them to participate in the activities of holiday times when family members get together. Very few Jehovah's Witnesses have a warm, loving, close relationship with family members who are not Witnesses. If a Jehovah's Witness decides to leave the organization, his or her so-called "Witness friends" and "Witness family members" are instructed to stay away from him and have nothing to do with him. Husbands are separated from wives, wives from husbands, children from parents, grandparents from children and grandchildren.

While the Jehovah's Witnesses claim to be against going to war and killing people with a gun, they have no qualms against putting people to death spiritually and socially, so to speak. They say that a disfellowshipped or even a disassociated Jehovah's Witness no longer has any contact with God, because one can only have contact with Him through the Watchtower Society. So the disfellowshipped Jehovah's Witness is completely ostracized from all his former acquaintances.

This is about the most severe punishment that can be inflicted upon a person. One can lose all material possessions and still survive with the support of family and friends; but to be considered socially dead and have no friends is very, very difficult. While teaching that God is a "God of love" and that the society is God's representative here upon this earth, it inflicts this cruel punishment on those who *dare* to question its authority. The Watchtower Society does not believe in a place of punishment—hell—in the next life, but it does believe in and practices putting former members through a figurative "hell" on earth.

Jehovah's Witnesses have absolutely nothing to do with "society in general." Watchtower publications constantly point out all the wickedness in the world, yet forbid members from doing anything to keep it from getting worse. The society does not allow the exercise of freedom of speech and choice. It does not allow members to vote in federal, state or local elections or participate in community activities. Instead, they stand on the sidelines and condemn everything in the world without offering a helping hand. Thus again, by its own definition, it would be considered a cult.

The article further defines a cult as a group whose "leaders are known to use manipulative methods to control the minds of their followers." If the society doesn't practice "mind control," why are Jehovah's Witnesses not allowed to read any religious books other than Watchtower publications? And why are they encouraged to read only *the most recent* Watchtower publications? If a Witness is reading too much of the "old stuff," the elders get suspicious and the person's motives will be questioned.

As Witnesses go door to door offering Watchtower literature, they are not allowed to receive any kind of literature in exchange—not even a short tract. In fact, they will even refuse to look at Watchtower literature! I recently saw a Jehovah's Witness crumple up and throw away, without ever looking at it, a page copied from a *Watchtower* magazine that came out only two months earlier. This was certainly not "old stuff"! (Often the Witness will call such material "apostate literature" without even looking at it.)

Why are Witnesses not allowed to talk to people who have studied the Watchtower Society thoroughly from an objective point of view? If the society taught its people discernment and did not manipulate them, it would allow its followers freedom to read what they wanted to read and talk to whomever they wanted to talk. If the society didn't consider itself vulnerable to honest criticism, it would not have to forbid its followers from reading other literature!

The article describes a cult as often meeting in secret,

and claims that Kingdom Hall meetings are open to the public. There are three points to make concerning this argument.

First of all, I question whether "secret" versus "public" meetings is a valid mark of a cult. While a few "cult" groups may have secret meetings, most of them also have meetings that are open to the public. And most organizations, including government agencies, have meetings that are not open to the public, such as executive meetings.

Second, while it is true that anyone may enter a Kingdom Hall, you dare not ask a thought-provoking question, or you will be promptly asked to leave. (I know, because it happened to me at a Kingdom Hall meeting. I asked a question about something that was said in the meeting to make sure I heard correctly; I was asked to leave, and when I did not, they called the police and had me thrown out.)

Third, though the five meetings a week held by the Jehovah's Witnesses are open to anyone, the *actual workings* of the Watchtower Society are kept secret, even to most Jehovah's Witnesses. An interesting statement is made in the preface to the 1945 book *The Jehovah's Witnesses* by Herbert Hewitt Stroup, published by Columbia University Press. When Mr. Stroup tried to objectively study the Watchtower Society in the process of writing a book, he ran into resistance from the organization's leaders. He wrote:

> Since the movement is in many ways a "secret" one, the members were loathe to give me openly any information. Moreover, the leaders issued orders to all local groups that I should not be aided in any direct way in securing my information. Even as late as November 1943, the present leader of the Witnesses, Mr. N.H. Knorr, informed me by letter that the "Society does not have the time,

nor will it take time, to assist you in your publication concerning Jehovah's witnesses. . . ." Aside from the scant material to be found in the brief *Yearbook*, "there is no other information that we have available to the public."

This makes it rather clear that the Watchtower Society is run in "secrecy." It is still done so today. Just try writing a letter or making a phone call to get any inside information and see what happens!

Another example of secrecy can be seen when charges are brought against an individual Jehovah's Witness and he or she is called before a "judicial committee." The accused person must appear alone; women as well as men must appear before three men (so much for a "jury of your peers"); and the hearing may not be recorded. (As far back as Old Testament times, a trial has been considered fair only if it is held openly, a public record is made of the hearing, and the accused is allowed to have defense counsel.) When this "judicial committee" finds a person guilty, only the verdict is announced to the congregation; no opportunity is given to the accused to explain his or her side. Why all the secrecy?

The Watchtower Society's finances are also kept in complete secrecy. No financial statement is provided. The average Jehovah's Witness is never told how much is made through literature or other donations to the society. Nor does the society reveal where it invests its money. Why are the finances such a secretive matter when the money comes from the rank and file among the Witnesses?

"Kingdom Hall Funds" are raised for the purpose of construction, yet it is estimated that in about forty percent of the cases, no new Kingdom Hall or addition is ever built. These funds are not returned to the donors but are put into a special fund to be used only by the governing body, and no accounting of these funds is ever given.

Most Witnesses are not aware of how the governing body is run. They do not realize that decisions are made by a vote and that a two-thirds majority is needed. (If the society is really "theocratic," why should the men on the governing body vote on what God has already told them?)

If the Watchtower Society does not do things in "secret," then why did it get so upset when the Norwegian edition of the book *Pay Attention to Yourself and Your Flock* turned up on the Internet in 1997? This is a book available only to elders; no one else is allowed to look at it. If there are no "secret" instructions given to elders, it should not have bothered the society that this book was made public.

One piece of vital information that has been kept a closely guarded secret is the spiritual status of Gerrit Losch, appointed to the governing body on July 1, 1994. In 1971, when the Watchtower Society changed from "one-man rule" to rule by a "governing body," the qualifications for those who would serve on this board were carefully spelled out in the December 15, 1971, *Watchtower*. We read:

> Let us keep in mind that the governing body must be made up of dedicated, baptized Christians who are anointed with God's spirit and begotten by him to be his spiritual children, and who are to be united with the glorified Jesus Christ in the heavenly kingdom.

The society teaches that a person had to be a baptized Witness before 1935 to be one of the "anointed"—one of the 144,000—and this was a qualification to be on the governing body. Today very few of those individuals are still alive, and all are very old. Was Gerrit Losch among that number? In the November 1, 1994, *Watchtower* we read:

GOVERNING BODY ADDITION. With a view of building up the personnel of the Governing Body of Jehovah's Witnesses, effective July 1, 1994, an additional member has been added to the 11 elders now serving. The new member is Gerrit Losch.

Brother Losch entered full-time service on November 1, 1961, and graduated from the 41st class of the Watchtower Bible School of Gilead. He served in the circuit and district work in Austria from 1963 to 1976. He married in 1967, and he and his wife, Merete, later served for 14 years as members of the Austria Bethel family in Vienna. Four years ago they were transferred to the Society's headquarters in Brooklyn, New York, where brother Losch has served in the Executive Offices and as an assistant to the Service Committee. With his varied experiences in the European field and his knowledge of German, English, Romanian, and Italian, he will make a valuable contribution to the work of the Governing Body.

Notice that not a single word is said about Gerrit Losch being one of the "anointed." The announcement speaks only of the experience he has had with the Watchtower Society.

Soon after the appointment of Gerrit Losch to the Governing Body, I heard about this and some of the details. I was anxious to know if he claimed to be one of the "anointed" or not. I wrote the following letter to the Watchtower headquarters.

August 20, 1994

Watchtower
25 Columbia Heights
Brooklyn, New York 11201

Dear Bethelite:

I am writing to you about some information I have heard about a new member being appointed to the governing body. I would like to know if what I heard is true and accurate.

I heard that Gerrit Losch, who is from Austria, was appointed to the governing body. Since he was born in 1941 and not baptized until 1959 then he could not be qualified as one of the "anointed," which we have been told for many years is an absolute necessity for being a member of the governing body.

I would like to know if this rumor is true or not. If it is a false rumor, then I want to have the facts and be able to present them so this does not go any further. However, on the other hand, if it is true, I do not want to speak against it.

I would appreciate your reply as soon as possible so that I will have the facts when I am asked or hear this information repeated.

Thank you very much.

Sincerely,

Wilbur Lingle

To my amazement I received the following letter in about two weeks. It generally takes at least six weeks to get an answer from the Watchtower Society, if you get an answer at all. I knew I had hit a sensitive issue since I received such a quick response!

EZM:ESE September 8, 1994

We are pleased to respond to your letter received August 25, 1994. We note your question about what you have heard concerning an addition of a new member to the Governing Body serving at the headquarters here in Brooklyn, New York.

As discussed in *The Watchtower* of February 1, 1982, a person's being of the anointed is a personal matter between that one and Jehovah God. It is not a matter concerning which a Christian may judge his brother. (Romans 14:10) It is true that since about 1935 the general call for spirit-anointed brothers of Jesus has ceased to go out. But, should one of the anointed prove unfaithful since that time and before having completed his earthly course, it is reasonable to conclude that his position would have to be filled by a replacement. In this regard, please note what is stated on page

383 of the June 15, 1970, issue of *The Watchtower*. In paragraph 1, it points out that favor would be given to the time-tested person over the novice in selecting such a replacement from among the 'great crowd.' This is especially reasonable in view of Jesus' statement to his disciples: "However, you are the ones that have stuck with me in my trials." (Luke 22:28) Brother Losch has been a dedicated servant of Jehovah for over three decades and professes to be of the anointed.

"This Governing Body," says the *Live Forever* book, page 195, "is made up of 'the faithful and discreet slave.' It serves as a spokesman for that faithful 'slave.'" All of them, then, are spirit-anointed Christians. The *Live Forever* book goes on to say: "The men of that Governing Body, like the apostles and older men in Jerusalem, have many years of experience in God's service." Be assured that Brother Gerrit Losch, recently appointed as a member of the Governing Body, meets these requirements.

We trust the above comments will be helpful to you. We send our warm love and Christian greetings.

Your brothers in Jehovah's service,

Notice that this letter is quite vague about the details as to when Gerrit Losch became one of the anointed, as they claim. (Contrary to what this letter implies, most of those who have claimed to be of the "anointed class" after 1935 have done so at the time of their baptism, when they were a novice, and not later on as they became more experienced. In fact, some who have claimed to be of the anointed at the time of baptism later on deny that they are one of the anointed.) I continued to hear reports that Gerrit Losch did not claim to be one of the "anointed," so I called the Brooklyn headquarters and talked to someone (who did not identify himself) for quite a long time. I tried to find out when Gerrit Losch first claimed to be one of the "anointed" and when he started taking the elements at the Memorial. I could not get any definite answers. Since this was such an important matter, I decided to write to Mr. Losch himself.

August 14, 1995

Mr. Gerrit Losch
25 Colombia Heights
Brooklyn, New YORK 11201-1698

Dear Mr. Losch:

I know that you are a very busy man but if you could help me clear up some rumors and confusion I would greatly appreciate it.

In the November 1, 1994, *Watchtower* where it announced your appointment to the governing body of Jehovah's Witnesses, on page 29 they wrote about the vast experiences that you have had that make you qualified to be a member of the governing body. In the article it did not mention anything about your being one of the "anointed." It has generally been reported that you are not one of the anointed. I have heard that people who know you personally say that you have never claimed to be one of the anointed. I talked to an elder on Saturday night and he was under the impression that you are not one of the anointed. However, I talked to a man in the Service Department there at Bethel and he said that you were one of the anointed. But when I asked him when you claimed to be one of the anointed, at baptism or later on, he could not give me any kind of an answer.

I think we ought to be truthful and it grieves me to hear these conflicting rumors going around. I go along with those who believe you are not one of the anointed. Would you please write to me and clear up the situation? If by some chance I am wrong and you are one of the anointed, would you tell me when you felt that you became one of the anointed?

Also there is another rumor going around—that about twenty years ago you were disfellowshipped. Would you also please comment on this?

I am sorry to bother you but I feel that the truth should be known so that these conflicting reports and rumors can be corrected.

Thank you very much for your prompt answer directly to me.

Sincerely,

Wilbur Lingle

I never received a reply to my letter. Whether Mr. Losch is one of the anointed or not is a *very important matter*. According to the Watchtower Society's own teachings, if he is not one of the "anointed," he does not have God's spirit and God cannot direct him into truth. I think Jehovah's Witnesses ought to know the spiritual standing of their own leaders.

The Watchtower Society, I have concluded, is not only run in secret to those who are outside but also to the Jehovah's Witnesses themselves. *They do not know how their own organization is run.*

As we have noted, it is quite evident from the Watchtower Society's own definition of a cult that they *used to be* a cult *if* they are not one now. But the question arises, *Is it possible for a cult to become a non-cult? And if so, how?* Such is a very rare happening.

It should be obvious that the Watchtower Society would have to admit that it used to be a cult and would have to completely repudiate all its previous actions, which it has never done. Also, it would have to acknowledge that for the first fifty years of its history, at least, it was deeply involved in "pagan" practices. The society has never acknowledged this either. But instead of confessing and repenting of its past, the society still *boasts* of its past, claiming that God has been using it from its inception in 1874 *and* that God chose it to be His "faithful and discreet slave" in 1919 when it was still cultistic and steeped in pagan practices.

Who Is "The Faithful and Discreet Slave"?

The Watchtower Society continually talks about "the faithful and discreet slave" as mentioned in Matthew 24:45-47 (NWT): "Who really is the faithful and discreet slave whom his master appointed over his domestics, to give them their food at the proper time? Happy is that slave if his master on arriving finds him doing so. Truly I say to you, He will appoint him over all his belongings." The society considers this slave to be the dispenser of God's truth to mankind on this earth. It believes that God *must* have an "organization" upon this earth, that there is only one *true* organization, and that *it* is that organization.

Originally, however, Charles Russell taught that *he* as an *individual* was the one whom God had appointed. He stated that he by himself was "the faithful and discreet slave." The succeeding two presidents of the Watchtower Society continued to have sole power and were considered, each in his time, to be "the faithful and discreet slave"—until the early 1970s. But during the third president's term, singular authority was wrested from N.H. Knorr by a group of men in the organization who then became known as the "governing body." As a result, the Watchtower Society now teaches that the entire "anointed remnant" making up the 144,000 left on earth are the "faithful and discreet slave," but that only the *governing body* is able to dispense spiritual food.

The Watchtower Society makes quite a few mistakes in its interpretation of this parable of "the faithful and discreet slave." It now teaches that God works only through an organization and will not reveal truth to individuals reading the Bible on their own. This ignores Jesus' promise in John 16:13:

> However, when that one [the Holy Spirit] arrives, the spirit of the truth, he will guide YOU [the Greek pronoun here is *plural* in form] into all the truth, for he will not speak of his own impulse, but what things he hears he will speak, and he will declare to YOU the things coming. (NWT)

The society further maintains that there is only one true, God-ordained organization—just like some other cults—at any particular time, and that the Watchtower Society is that one.

On what basis does the society claim that it is the only faithful group on earth? Simply by its own assertion. It makes a false assumption that in 1914 Michael set up his Kingdom in heaven and that it then was given authority over all other "slaves" because it had been the most faithful. But there is absolutely *no* evidence that the Kingdom was established in 1914.

We need to remember that prior to 1943 the Watchtower Society taught that the Kingdom was established in 1874. But now the society no longer teaches 1874 but 1914. It has had to admit that the 1874, date was erroneous. How do we know that the 1914 date will not soon be altered? Should that happen, the whole teaching about it being appointed the "faithful and discreet slave" would again be falsified.

The Watchtower Society is unique (except for a few Russellite splinter groups) in promoting the theory that the

Kingdom began in heaven in 1914; it is basing its claim upon its own private interpretation of Scripture and current events. Since it has had to change so many of its other interpretations and practices in the past, how can anyone be sure this interpretation will not also be altered?

Under the false assumption that the Kingdom was set up in 1914, the society teaches that from 1914 to 1919 Jehovah looked over all religious organizations at that time and, after five years of deliberation, chose the Watchtower Society as His "faithful and discreet slave." Let me give you the claim of the Watchtower Society in its own words, as taken from page 437 of the July 15, 1960, *Watchtower*.

> Of all the so-called Christian groups following World War I, only the awake witnesses of Jehovah were prepared to undertake the heavy global commission to preach the final witness. . . .
>
> Properly, then, to this 1900-year-old "faithful and discreet slave" with its thousands of cleansed "domestics" Jesus next says: "Truly I say to you [plural, collectively], He will appoint him over all his belongings." (Matt. 24:47) Those belongings are the interests of Christ's kingdom on earth. With practical wisdom Jesus entrusts these Kingdom interests to his veteran, proved "slave" class. Thus from 1919 forward this "slave" class, using the Watch Tower Society, has found itself in the unique position of responsibility and leadership concerning this kingdom, which it had previously heralded as to its coming, for over thirty years prior to 1914.

Thus, the Watchtower Society claims that it was the most faithful religious organization on the earth in 1919. Ironically, by the Watchtower Society's own admission, a large number of its 1919 beliefs and practices have since been discovered to be "pagan" and have been discarded. It begs the question: Why would Jehovah have selected a religious following that had so many "pagan" and "false" teachings?

And the 1919 date was significant because the prior year Joseph Rutherford, the president, and seven other officials of the Watchtower Society were incarcerated for things the society had published about World War I—statements that the U.S. government considered seditious. However, on March 25, 1919, the men were *released* from prison, and the society claims that *this* was a clear sign that God had set His approval upon the Watchtower Society. This became the basis for its claim of being the "faithful and discreet slave." Actually, it was nothing of the kind. The war was over, and the U.S. government simply saw no reason to keep these men in prison any longer.

Nowhere does the Bible teach that God works only through one organization. God has raised up many individuals to proclaim the truth. Organizations may have been formed around some outstanding men, but that is *not* a necessity for God to accomplish His plan. It is the Holy Spirit, using the Word of God, who leads true Christians into the accurate meaning of Scripture.

There is another serious problem concerning the Watchtower Society's claim that its "governing body" is the "faithful and discreet slave." The society teaches that all the men on the governing body must be among the 144,000 in order to be one of the "anointed." But *if* only 144,000 are "anointed," it would be impossible for any of them to be living in the twenty-first century. How so?

The Watchtower Society teaches that God began to choose the 144,000 right from the beginning of the church at the time of Pentecost. In the early church it has been estimated there were at least 250,000 Jews who were true Christians. In the Book of Acts at least 100,000 Christians are mentioned. Acts 21:20 reads in the Greek that there were "many tens of thousands" of Jews who were true believers. The Christian church spread rapidly among the Gentiles in the first century so there were hundreds of thousands of Christians. There were at least 250,000 Christians martyred under the Romans, and the Bible says the martyrs go to heaven and live and reign with Christ. Thus, the 144,000 would have been filled very shortly after the church began. So none of the "anointed" could be living today; thus the Watchtower is left without any authority.

Chapter Six

Two Classes of Witnesses

Many Jehovah's Witnesses and those studying with the Witnesses wonder when the policy of dividing members into an "elite *anointed* class" and a "second-rate *great crowd* class" (also known as the "other sheep") began.

In 1935 the Witnesses Were Divided

This happened in 1935. Up to that time, as we have noted, the society taught that all Jehovah's Witnesses would go to heaven. The 144,000 "anointed" were the "bride of Christ" and the "great crowd" would have a lesser standing and only be the guests of the bride, but they would all go to heaven. But in 1935 Rutherford changed this doctrine and taught that only 144,000 would go to heaven and the rest of the Witnesses, the "great crowd," would be second-class citizens and have to live on the new earth. Let us examine six advantages the "anointed" have over the "great crowd."

1. The "anointed" are supposed to possess and be di-

rected by God's Spirit, which enables them to interpret the Bible. The "great crowd" does not have God's Spirit and thus are said to be unable to understand the Bible on their own but have to be taught by "anointed" men on the governing body. Even though these men all supposedly are "anointed" and guided by God's Spirit, they still make many mistakes. However, the "other sheep" are less informed, so they don't have the opportunity to try to understand the Bible on their own.

2. The "anointed" are supposed to have a special sealing of the Spirit which enables them to endure persecution and trials more than the "other sheep." The Watchtower Society's teachings can offer no assurance of one's eternal destiny anywhere in the process of salvation, whether in this life or in the next, because all Jehovah's Witnesses must "endure to the end." There is always the possibility of "falling away," and 35% of Jehovah's Witnesses in America do. Therefore, this special sealing that the "anointed" are supposed to have gives them a great advantage over the "other sheep."

3. Only the "anointed" have a mediator.

4. According to Romans 8:8–11, only those who have God's Spirit can be in harmony with God and can please Him. Those who do not have God's Spirit are not in harmony with Him but are in "the flesh." They cannot please God. Since these "other sheep" don't possess God's Spirit directly, they are still in the flesh and displeasing to God.

5. The "anointed," supposedly with the heavenly calling, go to heaven, a place that God has prepared for them. But the "other sheep" are denied entrance into heaven and have to reside on an earth that they must rebuild by manual labor over a period of one thousand years.

6. Since only the "anointed" are supposed to be born of God, the "other sheep" can't be. However, according to First John 2:29, only those who are born of God can practice righteousness. And in First John 4:7 it states that only those who are born of God can truly experience love.

It is easy to see the vast advantages the "anointed" have over the "other sheep," according to the teachings of the Watchtower Society.

No Mediator for the "Great Crowd"

The Watchtower Society's teaching on who has a mediator is found in the April 1, 1979, *Watchtower* magazine. In the "Question from Readers" column, the following question is asked: "Is Jesus the 'mediator' only for anointed Christians?" The answer is "Yes." (The "anointed," remember, are made up only of those who were baptized into the Watchtower Society before 1935.) This means that all those Jehovah's Witnesses who make up the "great crowd" do *not* have anyone to mediate for them when they pray. When most Christians pray, they end their prayers by saying, "This we pray in the merits of the Lord Jesus Christ," or other words to that effect. But the "great crowd" of Jehovah's Witnesses cannot do this!

However, even those from the "anointed class," who claim to have a mediator, do not seem to have a very good one. The Watchtower Society states that Jesus Christ was annihilated at the time of His death, never to be seen again. It teaches that Jesus was raised as "a spirit" (which is J.W. "double-talk"). It actually means Michael the archangel (whom the society claims "willed himself out of existence" at the time of the birth of Christ) was recreated, and the name of the dead Jesus was just added on to his as one more of Michael's titles!

But Michael, of course, is only an angel. So the only live mediator even the anointed of the Jehovah's Witnesses could possibly have is an *angel*, who (according to their own publications) is a very poor mediator. In the 1982 Watchtower book *You Can Live Forever in Paradise on Earth* it states on page 125: "Angels have not faced such kind of testings. Nor have they experienced the problems common to humankind. So they would not fully understand what it is like to be a sinful human and to have the problems we humans do." So while the great crowd has no mediator at all, the anointed have a mediator who cannot perfectly understand them because Michael is only an angel. *What a sad condition to be in!*

The "Great Crowd" Cannot Produce the Fruit of the Spirit

The Watchtower Society teaches that only the "anointed" have God's spirit dwelling in them. Since the "great crowd" does not possess this, it is only natural to conclude that they cannot produce the "fruit of the spirit." If one is not walking in "the spirit," then one is walking in "the flesh," and thus producing the works of the flesh. Galatians 5:16 reads: "But I say, keep walking by the spirit and you will carry out no fleshly desire at all" (NWT).

The fruit of the Spirit is listed in Galatians 5:22–23: "Love, joy, peace, long-suffering, kindness, goodness, faith, mildness, self-control" (NWT). Thus, if any of these characteristics are found within the members of the "great crowd," it is something they are producing through the energy of the flesh.

Could this be the reason that there is so much backbiting, gossiping and bitter feelings among the Jehovah's Witnesses? Could this also be the reason why many Witnesses move from one congregation to another, hunting for love that is supposed to be among them without ever finding it?

Chapter Seven

The "New Earth" Problem

Watchtower publications abound with pictures of what the promised "new earth" will supposedly look like. There always seem to be mountains in the background, with rolling green hills, trees and beautiful flowers in the foreground, rounded out by a waterfall and lake. There are no roads, only pathways. Often there are groups of people from many nations dressed in their native costumes, which are mostly reserved for special occasions. Wild animals stand about and people are petting them. Usually there are baskets of delicious-looking fruits and vegetables in the pictures. Some illustrations show people enjoying an outdoor picnic. Occasionally there will be a group of men building a house. But these pictures are not realistic; they are merely an enticement to get people to join the Watchtower Society—and also to make the Witnesses happy with the many sacrifices they are currently making.

The Watchtower Society teaches that only 144,000 people will go to heaven. However, it claims that this number was completed in 1935, at which time the door to heaven was shut. The society now teaches that all the other Witnesses—the vast majority—will have to be satisfied with dwelling on Planet Earth. To attempt to prove this teaching, the society uses five verses from the Old Testament and one from the New. In Psalm 37, verses 9, 11, 22, 29 and 34 speak of those who "possess the earth." In Matthew 5:5 it speaks about "inheriting the earth."

But just as there is often a hidden agenda in many sales pitches, there is also one in the Watchtower Society's promise of Witnesses dwelling in a beautiful paradise on a new earth in the near future. The society teaches that before such a paradise can actually be realized, the world will be almost completely destroyed at Armageddon! This destruction will be produced by "cloudbursts, lashing rains, overflowing floods, earthquakes, giant hailstones, a rain of fire, etc."

Those who do not die in these horrible, natural disasters will either kill each other with swords or be dispatched by "a flesh-eating plague." God's angels will destroy those who remain. The society claims that only "faithful" Jehovah's Witnesses will escape with their lives, while the remaining six billion people on earth will be killed. So before a Witness can enjoy the new earth he must first witness the blood-curdling agony of billions of people dying from earthquakes, hurricanes, tidal waves, mass destruction and murder.

And there is another necessary scenario before a Witness can enjoy the promised paradise—one not ordinarily explained in any detail by the society. It pertains to the clean-up work that will be required after Armageddon. The first task that Jehovah's Witnesses must tend to is to dispose of the billions of dead bodies, both animal and human. Watchtower publications say, "Dead bodies will be ungathered, unburied, unwept for everywhere—from end to end of the earth." The society doesn't tell readers outright that the survivors will have to watch and gag while worms, birds and beasts swarm over these billions of decaying bodies until the last carcass is eaten up. Nor does it explain what happens to the trillions of swollen man-eating worms after this feast. Surely these flesh-eating worms will not continue to live on in paradise, will they? I have asked many Jehovah's Witnesses what will happen to these multiplied worms and the scavenging birds, but have never received any word of explanation. Nor have I read anything about this in any Watchtower publication.

However, the worms and birds cannot eat the bones, so the next duty of surviving Witnesses will be to gather up six billion ugly skeletons and bury them. This means that each Jehovah's Witness will, on the average, have to bury 1,100 skeletons. One Watchtower publication states that it will take the Witnesses "seven prophetic months" to bury all these skeletons. How revolting! And these bones must not be burned, because this new earth is declared to be a pollution-free earth—and burning human bones causes pollution. (I used to be a missionary in Japan, where they cremate the dead. In the city where I lived there was a crematorium that could consume eighty bodies at one time. There was always a noxious odor around this place.)

The next mind-boggling job for these "lucky" survivors will be to clear away by manual labor all the rubble of the millions and millions of destroyed houses, apartment buildings, skyscrapers, factories, stores, junkyards, graveyards, etc. (Visualize, if you will, a worldwide Katrina-like disaster.) It is only reasonable to assume that there will no longer be any functional mechanized equipment, nor any gasoline to run this equipment should it be found undamaged. Over the years I have asked Jehovah's Witnesses how this debris will be removed. I have never received any kind of reasonable answer. Some have replied, "Jehovah will dispose of it in some way."

But this answer does not agree even with Watchtower literature, because in the Watchtower book *You Can Live Forever in Paradise on Earth,* we read: "First of all, those who survive Armageddon will have the work of cleaning up the earth and clearing away the ruins of this old system." The Bible records no instance in which God gets rid of a destroyed civilization in a miraculous way, nor do we find any promises in the Bible that God will do so in the future. Consequently, this will be an overwhelming task that the surviving Jehovah's Witnesses will have to carry out themselves.

Since the Watchtower publications give no hint as to *how* the Witnesses will do this mammoth task, I always assumed it would happen with wheelbarrow and shovel. Later I found a picture in the Watchtower Society's 1992 thirty-two page brochure *Does God Really Care About Us?* which apparently proves my theory. On page 26 we see a picture of people cleaning up the destroyed earth, and sure enough it shows a young boy working with a wheelbarrow and shovel.

The Watchtower Society admits that the reconstruction of civilization is going to take a long time—1,000 years. At first, living conditions will be much worse than they are now. People will be far from perfect in their actions, and the physical body will still be plagued with many illnesses and infirmities. How people will maintain their health will be a very real problem.

Anyone associated with the Watchtower Society who knows their track record is aware that a college education is frowned upon. For this reason there are very few professional doctors and nurses among the Witnesses. So after Armageddon, who will assist medically? Many Jehovah's Witnesses will die for want of medication, because all pharmaceutical companies will have been destroyed. There will be no hospitals, clinics, medical supplies, testing devices, dialysis machines or oxygen tanks—and no electricity. The bulk of the world's accumulated medical knowledge will have been destroyed.

How are the Jehovah's Witnesses going to build up and reteach the survivors? Witnesses are a closed religious group run by men who have absolutely no experience in the medical field. It is easy for the Watchtower Society to come up with answers in an already-established, technically refined world, but it will be different in the face of reality after Armageddon.

Some Jehovah's Witnesses claim that not everything will be destroyed at Armageddon. Once again this answer does not agree with what is written in their 1995 book *KNOWLEDGE That Leads to Everlasting Life*, where we read about the new earth after Armageddon: "There will be plenty of enjoyable work to be done by Armageddon survivors. They will transform the earth into a paradise. *Any vestiges of the polluted old system will be cleared away. Parks and gardens will emerge in place of slums and ruined land*" [emphasis added].

However, it will surely be an impossible task to get rid of every vestige of pollution through manual labor! Have you ever driven past a house that is about to be torn down? There are three large trucks waiting to haul the debris away, as well as a bulldozer and a crane-like machine to load the refuse onto the trucks. And when you drive by hours later, they are still working. If it takes this long for just one house to be dismantled with mechanized equipment and dump trucks, what would it take for an entire demolished city to be cleared away by wheelbarrow and shovel? And where will all this debris be disposed of, since the Watchtower Society says that all the land must be used for living?

The Watchtower Society teaches that everyone on the new earth will be farmers who will grow their own vegetables and fruit, and raise cattle for meat. Obviously, at least a foot of topsoil will need to be spread over all these destroyed cities and towns where houses, factories, buildings, and roads once existed. But where will all this topsoil come from? The existing farmland will still be needed, so it can't be taken from there. I have never heard a Jehovah's Witness explain this point, and of course Watchtower publications never mention the problem.

In the 1988 Watchtower publication *INSIGHT on the Scriptures*, it is estimated that it will take at least a hundred years before enough of the old system is cleared away to allow for the dead to be resurrected onto this new earth. In fact, the Watchtower Society teaches that transforming the earth into a paradise is a *gradual process* which will involve the survivors for many generations. People will be far from perfect at the beginning of the Millennium, and environmental features will be transformed only gradually. This hard manual labor will continue for a thousand years.

Don't get the idea that the beautiful new earth, which is pictured in Watchtower publications, is what will be enjoyed for a thousand years. It is something that might be available at the very *end* of the thousand years—that is, if what the Watchtower Society speculates really proves true.

After six billion people are killed, eaten by worms and birds, the debris being mysteriously removed by wheelbarrow and shovel, and a foot of topsoil spread over all these destroyed areas—then and only then are the Witnesses ready to *begin* restoring the earth to a paradise-like condition. Just about every picture of the new earth presented in Watchtower publications shows men building Western-style homes with the type of lumber that is used today. They never portray log cabins or temporary huts or tents. But where is this nice, planed lumber going to come from?

I live in the eastern part of America. Trees that are big enough to be cut into lumber and used for homes are rare here. Most lumber comes from the West Coast. But remember, at this time there will be absolutely no commercial transportation like ships, trains or trucks, nor will there be adequate roads. And the preparation of all this lumber will have to be completed by hand. It takes electricity to run modern sawmills, but I have never seen a power plant pictured in any of the Watchtower publications, nor have I ever seen any power lines. But most power plants cause pollution—and the new earth is supposed to be pollution-free!

Then there is the question of where all the window glass, drywall, hardware, etc., that is needed to complete these houses comes from. There will be no hardware stores at this time. Again, this is a mystery that I have never had any Jehovah's Witness give me an answer for. How unrealistic are the glamorous pictures the Watchtower Society uses as bait to whet the appetite of those who read their publications!

At this point it is important to scrutinize the Watchtower Society's teaching on the original Garden of Eden. The society teaches that the Garden of Eden was a small site on the earth and not typical of the condition of the whole earth. If man had not sinned, he would still have had to go out and make the rest of the earth like the Garden of Eden through his own labor. It is only logical, then, for the Watchtower Society to conclude that this new earth is not something that *Jehovah* is going to produce in a miraculous way, but it is something that the dwellers on the new earth, *Jehovah's Witnesses*, will have to create.

The Bible says very clearly that during the thousand-year reign of Christ the inhabitants will have to do this work. Isaiah 65:21 in the New World Translation—a verse quoted often in Watchtower publications concerning the new earth—reads: "And they will certainly build houses and have occupancy; and they will certainly plant vineyards and eat [their] fruitage." Thus, when Jehovah's Witnesses give the glib answer that Jehovah God is going to work some kind of a miracle to make this earth a paradise, they are answering neither according to the Bible nor in line with the Watchtower Society's teachings.

If it is true that the world will be like the Garden of Eden after Armageddon, as the Watchtower Society teaches, will people be dressing in skins as did Adam and Eve, since all the clothing factories will have been destroyed? (I have searched in vain to find any factories in the pictures of this new earth that the Watchtower Society sets forth.) Will enough animals exist to provide the clothing they need? The people will have to live in crude dwellings and start all over again as Adam and Eve did—all from scratch. (Adam and

Eve had one distinct advantage, however: they didn't have billions of bones and mounds of rubble to dispose of!)

I have asked the above questions and presented the problems to a number of Jehovah's Witnesses. Their rather consistent answer is that these pictures are *only* an artist's concept and are not necessarily what the new earth will really look like. While talking to one Witness, I asked, "Isn't the Watchtower Society based solely on the Bible? If so, I would think that it would prohibit its artists from portraying any concepts not clearly found in the Bible. So why does the society print pictures which are probably far from an accurate representation of the new earth?" I didn't receive an answer. When I raised this question with another Witness he replied: "Maybe this is what the new earth will look like after eight or nine hundred years."

But one of the strangest things about this whole process is that the Jehovah's Witnesses will not be engaged in this hard manual labor for *just themselves* to enjoy. They will be building a beautiful new earth for all the billions of people who died before 1914 to also enjoy! And those masses destined to be resurrected include not just the righteous ones but *all* people, *good and bad*—everyone who lived and died before 1914.

The society has a double explanation for why this vast multitude is to be resurrected and given a fresh start on the new earth. First, it has concluded that Christ died only for the sins that we humans inherited from Adam—*these sins only*, and *not* for our personal sins. In short, the physical death that came upon all humankind because of Adam's sin is taken away in Christ—and this is automatic. No special faith is necessary.

Second, the society further theorizes that in 1914 the human race entered the "day of judgment," so the sacrifice that Christ made for Adam's sin no longer applies for people living today. The only way, since 1914, for a person to have a second chance to work for eternal life on the new earth is to die while in the good graces of the Watchtower Society, or to be living in the good graces of the society when Armageddon occurs. Hence the Watchtower Society claims to be doing the very work that, previous to 1914, was attributed to the work of Christ. (See page 183, paragraph 23 of the 1982 book *You Can Live Forever in Paradise on Earth.*) Therefore, the society teaches, *all* the people who lived before 1914 will be gradually resurrected and given a second chance on the new earth to work for and maybe merit eternal life—which means to have physical life in paradise.

The Bible clearly states, "The wages of sin is death" (Rom. 6:23). The society therefore declares, in the book just mentioned above, that when a person dies physically, he *pays for his own sins.* This qualifies him to be resurrected onto the new earth and given a fresh start. So the "lucky" Jehovah's Witnesses who happen to be alive when Armageddon comes have to experience all the horrors of watching the destruction of this old world system, observe the rotting bodies, bury the billions of bones, clear away all the scattered debris and endure all the hardships of restoring the earth to a normal, habitable condition—but will be doing this so that all the wicked people who died before 1914 can be resurrected and enjoy this beautiful new earth—a place that the Jehovah's Witnesses spent hundreds of years to build.

The Watchtower Society further teaches that death (annihilation) is just like falling asleep and is a condition where there is no kind of feeling, which means no suffering. So these wicked people have personally suffered nothing.

In truth, the Watchtower Society has things reversed. If the wicked had to experience all the horrors of Armageddon and had to do all the work for the "righteous," I might be able to understand that; but for the so-called "righteous" to have to experience all this horror and work for hundreds of years so all the wicked people of the world could enjoy a new life, seems untenable.

However, there are still other problems pertaining to this new earth promised by the Watchtower Society. As we have just mentioned, the society teaches that when a person dies he pays the wages for his inherited sin. This entitles him to a fresh new start on the new earth, even though he still will not be perfect. Remember, the Watchtower Society teaches that Armageddon is just around the corner; so most of the Jehovah's Witnesses living today presume that they will not die, but rather will go directly into the new earth without ever tasting death.

But here is the snag: When do individual Jehovah's Witnesses pay the wages for *their* inherited sin? I have asked a number of Jehovah's Witnesses this question but have never received an answer. But this query usually causes them to admit that at the beginning of the new earth the moral condition will be *very little different* than what it is in this present wicked world! The Witnesses also explain that making the destroyed earth into a paradise, both physically and *morally*, will be a lengthy process— drawn out over a thousand years.

Even though all those who died before 1914 supposedly paid for their inherited sins when they died, they were still not perfect when they died; so they will not be perfect when they are resurrected. As a result, the society says that they will have to be educated concerning Jehovah so that they may choose to reject or to conform to Him. The society estimates that it will probably take at least 300 years to gradually resurrect the estimated 20 to 22 billion people who have lived on this earth. But these people must be instructed. Besides all the backbreaking labor of rebuilding this destroyed earth, the Jehovah's Witnesses will also have to conduct so-called "Bible studies" with these resurrected people to give them the opportunity to accept or to reject Jehovah's teachings.

The society estimates that this process will take from 100 to 500 years. If these people respond to these teachings, they can continue to live on the new earth and have the opportunity to work so that they *might* merit eternal life at the end of the thousand years. But if they refuse to respond to Jehovah's teachings—refuse, that is, to become Jehovah's Witnesses—they will be annihilated.

But in order for these people to be annihilated, they must, of course, die. But the Watchtower Society says that on the restored earth there will be no sickness or aging, and death will no longer exist! It also declares that there will be no graveyards and thus no need for undertakers. Since people will not grow old, get sick or die, how then will these unresponsive people be put to death in order to reach the state of annihilation? I have never received a reasonable answer from a Jehovah's Witness as to how this will be accomplished.

The only way I know to put these people to death would be for God Himself to destroy them. We have an example of this in Leviticus 10:1–5. The two sons of Aaron, Nadab and Abihu, offered illegitimate fire upon the altar and the Bible says, "Fire came out from before Jehovah and consumed them, so that they died before Jehovah" (NWT). However, the bodies were still left and had to be removed and buried. So even when recalcitrant people on the new earth are "consumed," their bodies will remain. Since there are no graveyards or undertakers, how then will these bodies be disposed of?

And here are two additional problems about this grand new earth that must be faced: Assuming that the Watchtower Society's promise about the new earth is true, is there any guarantee that the Jehovah's Witnesses who get there will be able to reside there forever? The society claims that, after having been annihilated a thousand years previously, Satan will be recreated for a brief period to tempt people at the end of the Millennium. A large multitude will follow Satan in his rebellion and be eternally annihilated. It is even possible that many faithful Witnesses may fall away—after hundreds of years of faithfulness and hard labor!

And those who survive will not be in a very rosy situation. Satan will declare war on Michael, so again there will be wide destruction of buildings and people—which will once more have to be disposed of. So all the laborious effort these Witnesses put forth in building the new earth will come to naught and they will have to start all over again!

Thankfully, the idea of God's people building a paradise on earth in which to live forever is not taught in the Bible—just the opposite, in fact. First Thessalonians 4:13–18 tells us that those who have faith in the Lord Jesus Christ as their personal Savior will go to heaven when Christ returns, to a perfect place which God Himself has built. Jesus said in John 14:1–3 (NWT),

Do not let your hearts be troubled. Exercise faith in God, exercise faith also in me. In the house of my Father there are many abodes. Otherwise, I would have told you, because I am going my way to prepare a place for you. Also, if I go my way and prepare a place for you, I am coming again and will receive you home to myself, that where I am you also may be.

Chapter Eight

Strange Ideas about Holidays, Birthdays, the Lord's Supper and Blood Transfusions

There are a number of Watchtower teachings in which apparently innocuous practices have been elevated to the level of mortal sin. For example, Jehovah's Witnesses are very vocal about condemning all holidays and birthdays. They even go so far as to state that anyone who observes holidays or birthdays cannot be a true Christian. Of course, if this is true, then there were not any true Jehovah's Witnesses until after 1928, because until that time Jehovah's Witnesses did indeed observe these things. (Surely the organization would not have a double standard!)

Holidays Are Not "Pagan"

In the 1993 Watchtower publication *Jehovah's Witnesses— Proclaimers of God's Kingdom*, consider these important remarks concerning holidays and birthdays:

R. H. Barber, a member of the headquarters staff who made a thorough investigation of the origin of Christmas customs and the fruitage that these were yielding, presented the results in a radio broadcast. That information was also published in *The Golden Age* of December 12, 1928. It was a thorough exposé of the God-dishonoring roots of Christmas. . . .

. . . and the spirit in which many gifts were given did not honor God; that the magi whose gift-giving was being imitated were actually demon-inspired astrologers. . . .

Jehovah's Witnesses enjoy good times with their families and friends. But they do not participate in holidays and celebrations that are linked with pagan gods (as is true of such holidays as Easter, New Year's Day, May Day, and Mother's Day). (2 Cor. 6:14-17) Like the early Christians, they do not even celebrate birthdays. They also respectfully refrain from sharing in national holidays that memorialize political or military events and refrain from giving worshipful honor to the national heroes. Why? Because Jehovah's Witnesses are not part of the world.

There are a number of statements in this quote that need to be challenged. It is generally understood that a "root" is the very source or beginning of something. Note what was written: "It was a thorough exposé of the God-dishonoring *roots* of Christmas." If this article had said "God-dishonoring practices that have built up around Christmas," that would have been a vast difference in meaning. But the article used the word "roots."

What is the "root" of Christmas? What is the primary purpose of celebrating it? Is it not to remember the birth of the Lord Jesus Christ, who came into this world as the very Son of God? The "roots" of Christmas therefore cannot be "pagan," because they are born out of the truth of Christ's birth as found in the Bible! The Watchtower Society argues that it is "pagan" to celebrate Christmas. But *celebrate* means "to rejoice." Are we to not rejoice over the birth of the Lord Jesus Christ?

The Watchtower Society claims to be based solely on the Bible. I would challenge any Jehovah's Witness to prove *just from the Bible* that Christmas is a "pagan" holiday and so should not be observed. We do find that the birth of the Lord Jesus Christ was celebrated in the Bible. The details are found in Luke 2:8–20. Since this is such an important part of Scripture, I would like to quote this passage using the *New World Translation* (NWT), with the verse numbers in the text:

> 8. There were also in that same country shepherds living out of doors and keeping watches in the night over their flocks. 9. And suddenly Jehovah's angel stood by them, and Jehovah's glory gleamed around them, and they became very fearful. 10. But the angel said to them: "Have no fear, for, look! I am declaring to you good news of a great joy that all the people will have, 11. because there was born to you today a Savior, who is Christ [the] Lord, in David's city. 12. And this is a sign for you: you will find an infant bound in cloth bands and laying in a manger." 13. And suddenly there came to be with the angel a multitude of the heavenly army, praising God and saying: 14. "Glory in the heights above to God, and upon earth peace among men of good will." 15. So when the angels had departed from them into heaven, the shepherds began saying to one another: "Let us by all means go clear to Bethlehem and see this thing that has taken place, which Jehovah has made known to us." 16. And they went with haste and found Mary as well as Joseph, and the infant lying in the manger. 17. When they saw it, they made known the saying that had been spoken to them concerning this young child. 18. And all that heard marveled over the things told them by the shepherds, 19. but Mary began to preserve all these sayings, drawing conclusions in her heart. 20. Then the shepherds went back, glorifying and praising God for all the things they heard and saw, just as these had been told them.

(Note carefully that in verse 17 the Watchtower Society's translation referred to the very Son of God, Jesus Christ, as "it." There is no rhyme or reason for the pronoun to be rendered "it" instead of "him.")

You will notice that it was God Himself who announced the birth of His Son—and He announced it with not just one angel, but a "multitude." If the Father celebrated the birth of His Son in such a glorious way, why should it be considered improper for true followers of Christ to imitate the Father and rejoice at the birth of Christ?

Jehovah's Witnesses respond to this question by saying we should be thankful every day. I too believe this, but that need not prevent us from being especially thankful for the birth of our Savior once a year. Besides, this argument cuts both ways. Even though Jehovah's Witnesses do not observe His birth once a year, they do observe His death annually at their Memorial. Shouldn't we be thankful for the death of Christ every day?

The Watchtower Society further argues that we are nowhere commanded to celebrate the birth of Jesus Christ. This is true; but neither are we told we *can't* remember the birth of our Savior. Surely to pause and think about the birth of Christ on a certain day is not disobedience to God, for the custom of remembering the birth of Christ was not derived from paganism. And since God the Father spotlighted the birth of His Son, following this example of the Father certainly cannot be "pagan."

All the society's arguments against observing Christmas and other holidays come from encyclopedias, not the Bible. The Watchtower's 1989 publication *Reasoning from the Scriptures,* under the heading of "Holidays," contains ten quotes taken from encyclopedias and three from other sources. This book (in contrast to its title, ironically) does not quote a single Bible verse to prove their claim that it is wrong to remember the birth of Jesus Christ on a certain day.

The main reason the Watchtower Society rejects Christmas has to do with the date, December 25. The society cites encyclopedias that claim Emperor Constantine changed the date for observing Christmas to December 25 in order to coincide with the Roman Saturnalia, a festival dedicated to the Roman god Saturn. But the sources used are hardly conclusive. The *Reasoning* book quotes *The Encyclopedia Americana* which admits, "The reason for establishing December 25 as Christmas is somewhat obscure, but is usually held . . ." The book also quotes from the *New Catholic Encyclopedia* which reads, "According to the hypothesis suggested by H. Usener . . ." So while the book uses encyclopedias to try to prove pagan roots for the date on which we celebrate Christmas, it blatantly ignores the encyclopedias' use of such words as "somewhat obscure" and "hypothesis."

Such a weak argument is no proof that Christmas has a pagan origin. But even if the "hypothesis" were true—that the date for Christmas was changed to December 25 to coincide with the Roman Saturnalia festival—the very fact that it was changed means that Christmas was observed before this time. You can't change the date of a holiday that didn't already exist! Their argument only proves that Christmas was indeed observed in the early church.

The only biblical argument ever raised for the day of Christ's birth not being December 25 is that in Luke 2: Sheep and shepherds were in the fields, and December would have been too cold for shepherds to be outside. This is a poor argument for two reasons: First, the average temperature of the Jerusalem area is between 45 and 59 degrees in December (*National Geographic Atlas of the World*, Fourth Ed. [1975], p. 193)—hardly unbearable, especially if the shepherds had campfires to keep warm. Second, because sheep had to be available for sacrifice in the temple at all times, some sheep and shepherds had to be in the fields year round.

It has been suggested that these shepherds may have been keeping watch over the very sheep that were to be sacrificed in the temple. This vision of angels, then, would have special significance to them, because they were looking for "the Lamb of God" who would be the ultimate sacrifice to take away the "sin of the world." They knew that once He Himself came, there would be no more need for animal sacrifices.

There may also be another explanation for why this date was chosen to celebrate the birth of Christ: The temple in Jerusalem was desecrated in 168 BC, then rededicated three years later on the same date—December 25! So the birth of Christ was set on the same day as the rededication of the temple. There is some evidence that Christmas was celebrated on December 25 as far back as the New Testament era (see *Chronological Aspects of the Life of Christ*, Zondervan, 1979).

Another objection the Watchtower Society has against Christmas is the custom of gift-giving. They claim that giving gifts at Christmas was started by the magi who gave gifts to the baby Jesus—and true Christians should not follow the example of the magi, who were "actually demon-inspired astrologers"!

First of all, the custom of giving gifts to one another at Christmas may not necessarily be following the example of the magi. While the magi did bring gifts, it wasn't actually at the time of Christ's birth. It is well known from the Bible that the magi came some time after Jesus was born. But even if the custom did come from them, why does the Watchtower want to paint the magi in such an evil light, when the Bible speaks so positively of them?

This objection is nothing more than another cheap attempt to try to put a "pagan" label on Christmas. It is hard to understand how any "demon-inspired astrologers" would have the discernment to understand that the special star they saw in the sky would lead them to the "King of the Jews" (the Jews were a despised people at that time), and then make all the preparations for such a long and dangerous trip, search so diligently for this new-born King, offer Him such extravagant gifts, and ultimately bow down and worship this young child!

It is difficult to believe that God would lead any "demon-inspired astrologers" in this way, and that Satan would lead his followers to come and worship the Lord Jesus Christ! If these really had been "demon-inspired astrologers," surely Satan would have led them back to King Herod so he could have killed the baby Jesus right away. Why did these magi listen to the warning given to them in a dream from God to return another way? It seems strange that "demon-inspired astrologers" would be so sensitive to the leading of the true God of the Bible.

Surely this demonstrates the lengths to which the Watchtower Society will go in order to keep people from celebrating the greatest event in history. Jesus Christ left all of heaven's glory to be born into this world, in order that He might die and shed His precious blood for the sins of mankind. Now man no longer has to bear the burden of his own sin. He has the opportunity of forgiveness through a personal faith in the Lord Jesus Christ as his divine Savior.

Apparently the writers of the Watchtower Society's publications are not aware that the Bible does speak about banqueting, rejoicing and gift-giving—from which we might get our custom of giving gifts at Christmastime. In the book of Esther, to commemorate the time when the Jews were kept from being slaughtered, the Feast of Purim was established. In Esther 9:22 we read:

> According to the days on which the Jews had rested from their enemies and the month that was changed for them from grief to rejoicing and from mourning to a good day, to hold them as days of banqueting and rejoicing and sending of portions to one another and of gifts to the poor people.

Since the early Christian church was made up of hundreds of thousands of converted Jews, might not the custom of giving gifts in remembrance of the birth of Jesus Christ be a carry-over from the custom at the Feast of Purim?

Other Christmas customs that have a Christian basis have never been mentioned by the Watchtower Society. The evergreen tree used at Christmas stands for the eternity of the Son of God. The candles stand for the fact that Jesus is the "Light of the world." The Watchtower Society completely overlooks these positive commemorative symbols.

Today's Jehovah's Witnesses would be shocked if they were bold enough to read what their leaders once taught. Consider what Charles Russell and Joseph Rutherford (for the first ten years of his presidency) thought about Christmas and observing it on December 25. Here are five excerpts from letters they wrote:

This review is perhaps as appropriate a lesson for the closing Sunday of the year as any, especially when we remember that all of these glories and blessings and privileges are ours because of the great redemptive work accomplished by him whose entrance upon the work is celebrated by Christmas day. Although we cannot agree that this is the proper day for celebrating the birth of our dear Redeemer, but must insist that it was about October first, nevertheless since he did not intimate his desire that we should celebrate his birth it is quite immaterial upon what day that event, of so great importance to all, is celebrated. Upon this day, so generally celebrated, we may properly enough join with all whose hearts are in the attitude of love and appreciation toward God and toward the Savior. (*The Watch Tower*, Dec. 15, 1903, p. 457)

Even though Christmas day is not the real anniversary of our Lord's birth, but more properly the annunciation day or the date of his human begetting (Luke 1:28), nevertheless, since the celebration of our Lord's birth is not a matter of divine appointment or injunction, but merely a tribute of respect to him, it is not necessary for us to quibble particularly about the date. We may as well join with the civilized world in celebrating the grand event on the day which the majority celebrate—"Christmas day." (*The Watch Tower*, Dec. 1, 1904, p. 364) [Note that it was the "civilized world" that celebrated the birth of Christ and not the "pagan world."]

It might interest you to know that we are already offering the books for "Christmas gifts." We find that many secure their Christmas presents several months ahead. . . . (*The Watch Tower*, Nov. 15, 1907, p. 351)

A Message of Gratitude
To the Dear Friends everywhere:
—Grace, mercy and peace be multiplied unto you!

Am taking advantage of an opportunity to dictate this note to extend to all the dear friends throughout the United States and Canada my heartfelt thanks for the great love bestowed upon us and manifested in the numerous Christmas presents which I and my associates have received, as well as cards, letters and messages of love. May the Lord bless you one and all!

I am unable to write you personally and so am asking that this general message be given you. I am overwhelmed by your expressions of love, dear brethren. May the Lord reward you richly!

Your brother and servant by his grace,

J.F. Rutherford
(*The Watch Tower*, Jan. 15, 1919, p. 31)

Students of the Scriptures also know that the birth of the babe Jesus did not take place in December; yet because of the general belief upon this point by most people, it seems to be an appropriate time to speak the truth concerning his birth and the purpose thereof. The Scriptural testimony, supported by extraneous facts, shows that the birth of Jesus occurred approximately October 1st. The event is so important that it is always appropriate to call it to the minds of the people, regardless of the date. (*The Watch Tower*, Dec. 15, 1926, p. 371) [I would like to know exactly *where* in the Bible is the "Scriptural testimony" which "shows that the birth of Jesus occurred approximately October 1st."]

But what about other holidays? The society states that Mother's Day is "linked with pagan gods." But in pagan lands, mothers are not held in high esteem. Mother's Day was started by a godly American woman to do what the Bible commands: to honor mothers.

In Exodus 20:12, we are commanded: "Honor your father and your mother in order that your days may prove long upon the ground that Jehovah your God is giving you" (nwt). This cannot be passed off as being a command in just the Hebrew Scriptures and no longer necessary, as the Watchtower Society often does with other commands it does not like. This same injunction is repeated in the Greek Scriptures in Ephesians 6:2: "'Honor your father and [your] mother': which is the first command with a promise" (NWT).

Thus, it is irrational to say, as the Watchtower Society does, that Mother's Day is "linked with pagan gods."

Even if the Watchtower Society were to find some place in the world where pagans do honor mothers on a certain day of the year, it would still not negate the clear command of *God* to honor mothers. Just because some pagans practiced a command found in the Bible does not make it pagan and an excuse for a person not to obey the command of the Bible.

Many times the excuse used by a Jehovah's Witness for not observing Mother's Day once a year is "We should be thankful every day for our mothers." I agree—I should be thankful every day—but that doesn't make a special day every year to remember mothers "pagan"!

Thanksgiving Day is one holiday I would challenge any Jehovah's Witness to prove is pagan. This holiday was started in America by the Pilgrims to thank the God of the Bible for His care and His many material blessings. Since these God-fearing people were familiar with the Bible, they knew that in the Hebrew Scriptures God had set aside one week every year as a time of celebration to thank Him for all the material blessings He had bestowed. This is called the "Feast of Booths" or "Feast of Tabernacles" and is found in Deuteronomy 16:13–15.

The Watchtower Society tries to explain this away by saying this command was given in the Hebrew Scriptures, and since we are no longer under the Old Testament laws it doesn't apply to us. (This is is rather hypocritical, however; when there is no apparent proof for its teachings and practices from the New Testament, the society has no qualms about using Old Testament verses as "proof texts.")

In the *Awake* magazine, November 22, 1976, the society wrote this about New Testament Jewish Christians who were still observing the "Feast of Tabernacles": "These former Jews were clinging to religious observances that God no longer desired." Is the Watchtower Society saying that God no longer desires His followers to be thankful for the material blessings that He gives?

Thanksgiving Day in America is generally thought of as a day to pause and thank God for all His material blessings. What is wrong with a nation stopping and being reminded that God is still in control of the world and is the One who supplies all our physical needs? The date on which Thanksgiving has been observed has been changed many times, so there cannot be any "pagan roots" for the day on which it is observed.

While most Jehovah's Witnesses would not think of observing Thanksgiving Day on the fourth Thursday of November, many *do* have a special day in November when they eat turkey and all the other kinds of food that others enjoy on Thanksgiving Day. What is the difference?

When presented with the true facts of the origin of holidays which are based on truths found in the Bible, Jehovah's Witnesses will repeat Second Corinthians 6:17 (NWT): "'Therefore get out from among them, and separate yourselves,' says Jehovah, 'and quit touching the unclean thing, and I will take you in.'" I thoroughly agree that Christians should separate from worldly practices, but the Watchtower Society needs to first convince me that observing a special day in order to be thankful to God for material blessings is "pagan" and not biblical before this verse can apply to this situation.

An important article on what to observe and what to shun because of its past association is found in the December 22, 1976, *Awake.* Consider these portions of the article:

> What should be a Christian's attitude toward shapes and designs that have at some time or place been connected with false religion? . . . For instance, the Winged Globe or Winged Disk was used in various forms in Phoenicia, Assyria and other nations. [The Watchtower Society used this Winged Globe design on the covers of a number of the seven books in the series known as *Studies in the Scriptures.*]

> Snakes, crosses, stars, birds, flowers . . . yes, there is an almost endless number of designs and symbols that have at some time or other been linked with idolatrous worship. So how can the sincere Christian know what to avoid and what to overlook as unimportant? . . .

> Just because idol worshipers at some time or place might use a certain design that does not automatically mean that true worshipers must always shun it. For instance, figures of palm trees, pomegranates and bulls were incorporated in the design of Jehovah's temple in Jerusalem. The fact that other religions might take these natural things that God created and use them as symbols in idol worship did not make it wrong for true worshipers to use them decoratively. Anyone visiting the temple could tell that God's people were not worshiping these decorations or venerating them as sacred symbols.

> Many times a design will change in significance according to location and time. A certain shape may have a particular meaning to an observer at one time and place, but a different meaning to an observer elsewhere or in another age. . . . Those past religious meanings do not readily come to the mind of most observers today. . . . *A pagan religious symbol might lose its religious connotation.*

> In yet other places neither of these significances may generally come to mind. . . . So the Christian needs to be primarily concerned about what? Not what a certain symbol or design possibly

meant thousands of years ago or how it might be thought of on the other side of the world, but what it means now to most people where he lives. . . .

But, as another example, let us return to the heart-shape [mentioned in the beginning of the article]. Though this was a religious symbol in ancient Babylon, does it now have such a meaning where you live? Most likely not. . . .

With so many different designs having been used in false worship, if a person went to the trouble and took the time he might find an undesirable connection with almost every design he sees around him. But why do that? Would it not be needlessly upsetting? And is that the best use of one's time and attention? . . .

Paul, however, also showed the value of concentrating on the things that are of real importance instead of getting involved in controversy over petty meanings and possible connections that are not of obvious significance.

The Watchtower Society doesn't follow its own advice when it comes to holidays. It doesn't matter what holiday it is, in what country of the world, the society "went to the trouble and took the time" to try to associate *every* holiday with some pagan background. Also the society does not let any of the holidays discard their past and have a different meaning for those who observe them today. There are very few people who associate Christmas, Thanksgiving Day, Mother's and Father's Day, or Resurrection Day with anything pagan. In the minds of most people, these are Christian observances and have nothing to do with anything "pagan."

Why does today's Watchtower Society become so upset over people practicing what its followers participated in for nearly fifty years? If observing holidays is condemned so plainly in the Bible, why did it take these "Bible Students" fifty years to discover this?

If Jehovah's Witnesses do not want to observe holidays, so be it, but they should not condemn what God does not condemn! Witnesses should take the advice of the Bible as found in Romans 14:1–12 (NWT):

> Welcome the [man] having weaknesses in [his] faith, but not to make decisions on inward questionings. One [man] has faith to eat everything, but the [man] who is weak eats vegetables. Let the one eating not look down on the one not eating, and let the one not eating not judge the one eating, for God has welcomed that one. Who are you to judge the house servant of another? To his own master he stands or falls. Indeed, he will be made to stand, for Jehovah can make him stand.

> One [man] judges one day as above another; another [man] judges one day as all others; let each [man] be fully convinced in his own mind. He who observes the day observes it to Jehovah. Also, he who eats, eats to Jehovah, for he gives thanks to God; and he who does not eat does not eat to Jehovah, and yet gives thanks to God. None of us, in fact, lives with regard to himself only, and no one dies with regard to himself only; for both if we live, we live to Jehovah, and if we die, we die to Jehovah. Therefore both if we live and if we die, we belong to Jehovah. For to this end Christ died and came to life again, that he might be Lord over both the dead and the living.

> But why do you judge your brother? Or why do you also look down on your brother? For we shall all stand before the judgment seat of God; for it is written: "As I live," says Jehovah, "to me every knee will bend down, and every tongue will make open acknowledgment to God." So, then, each of us will render an account for himself to God.

If Birthdays Are "Pagan," What about Abraham?

The society now claims that observing birthdays is a "pagan" custom even though Witnesses observed birthdays for over fifty years. But if this practice is really "pagan," then the great patriarch of the nation of Israel, Abraham, would have to be considered a pagan, because he had a birthday party for Isaac. In Genesis 21:8 (NWT) we read: "Now the child kept growing and came to be weaned; and Abraham then prepared a big feast on the day of Isaac's being weaned." Studying ancient foreign cultures teaches us that children were often weaned from their mother's breast when they were three or fours years old. We note that Abraham had a feast for Isaac "on the *day* he was weaned." So this was probably Isaac's third or fourth birthday. Thus, Abraham did have a birthday party for Isaac. Is the Watchtower Society willing to say that Abraham was "pagan" because he had a birthday party for his son?

The society's condemnation of all birthdays is based on only two biblical passages. One is Matthew 14:1–11 where John the Baptist was beheaded as a result of Herod's birthday party. The other is Genesis 40:20–22, where we read that the chief baker was hanged on Pharaoh's birthday. The society claims that since two people were killed on these birthdays, all birthday celebrations are "pagan."

But there is one twist to Pharaoh's birthday feast that the Watchtower Society apparently has never considered (or doesn't want to): Though the chief baker was hanged on Pharaoh's birthday, the chief butler was restored to his former position—and it was the chief butler who told Pharaoh about Joseph (see Gen. 41). And because Pharaoh learned about Joseph, a great famine was averted and Joseph was reconciled with his brothers. This important event in the plan and purpose of God occurred because of what transpired at Pharaoh's birthday feast. So it is not correct to say that *only* evil things happened on the two birthdays mentioned in the Bible! No, the Bible does not condemn birthdays.

The Watchtower Society argues that "men" are honored when we celebrate birthdays and we should not honor men. However, the Bible often recognizes and honors people, and the society cannot cite any biblical principle not to do this. In addition, Jehovah's Witnesses have graduation parties where graduates are honored; anniversaries where married couples are honored; and wedding receptions where newly married couples are honored What is the difference? Why is it wrong to honor people on their birthdays but acceptable to honor them at graduations, weddings and anniversaries?

By the way, if it is "pagan" for an individual to have a birthday party, shouldn't it be "pagan" for an organization to have one? The Watchtower Society celebrated the one hundredth birthday of the *Watchtower* magazine, as noted in the *Kingdom Ministries* of July 1979!

The Lord's Supper

When Jehovah's Witnesses are challenged about observing holidays or birthdays, they will often say, "We should be thankful every day and not just one day a year." But this argument completely falls apart when it comes to their observance of the Lord's Supper, or the Breaking of Bread. The following is a quote on this subject from the November 22, 1976, *Awake*:

> However, with the teachings of Jesus Christ came a new view of the prescribed Jewish celebrations. Just before his death, Jesus commanded but one celebration. He required his followers to memorialize his death. This observance was made all the more outstanding by its being the only one. (Luke 22:19-20)

Jehovah's Witnesses observe the Memorial only once a year. Using the Jewish calendar, they put it on Nisan 14, which is the day of the Jewish Passover. According to our calendar, it would fall between March 26 and April 25.

As to how often the Memorial should be observed, the Watchtower Society says in its book *Reasoning from the Scriptures*:

> Jesus did not specifically state how often it was to be done. He simply said: "Keep doing this in remembrance of me." (Luke 22:19) Paul said: "For as often as you eat this loaf and drink this cup, you keep proclaiming the death of the Lord, until he arrives." (1 Cor. 11:26) "As often" need not mean many times a year; it can mean annually over a period of many years.

Since the Watchtower Society claims that the Memorial is the only ceremony we are commanded to fulfill, then it ought to be carried out according to the Bible. As noted above, however, when Witnesses are asked why they don't observe other holidays once a year, they reply, "We should be thankful every day." If this is true, then shouldn't Christ's death be remembered every day by means of the Memorial? When I have asked Jehovah's Witnesses why they don't observe the Memorial more often, they reply, "If you do something too often, there is the tendency for it to become commonplace." Why these contradictions in their explanations?

The first incidence in the Bible of the Memorial being observed after the death and resurrection of Jesus Christ is found in Acts 2:42 and 46. It reads as follows:

> And they continued steadfastly in the apostles' doctrine and fellowship, and *in breaking of bread*, and in prayers. . . . And they, continuing daily with one accord in the temple, and *breaking bread*

from house to house, did eat their meat with gladness and single-ness of heart. (KJV)

So it was observed "daily." Therefore if the Watchtower Society was following the Bible, it would have its members observe the Memorial frequently. But not only does the Watchtower Society not follow the biblical pattern, but it has changed the wording in its *New World Translation* of the Bible so that its followers will not realize that Communion was observed daily by the earliest Christians. Note carefully how the NWT reads in Acts 2:42 and 46.

And they continued devoting themselves to the teaching of the apostles and to sharing [with one another], *to taking of meals* and to prayers. . . . And day after day they were in constant attendance at the temple with one accord, and they *took their meals in private homes* and partook of food with great rejoicing and sincerity of heart.

There is a footnote in the 1984 large reference edition of the NWT which refers to "to taking of meals" in verse 42 which reads, "Lit., 'to the breaking of the bread.'" The words for "taking of meals" are entirely different Greek words from "breaking of bread." So why did the Watchtower Society use a different wording in the text and only note the proper ren-dering of it in a footnote? Apparently this is something it does not want its followers to be aware of!

Also in verse 46 we read "and they took their meals." Again, instead of using the proper phrase for "breaking of bread," which refers to the taking of communion, it states "and they took their meals." In fact, the NWT is even re-dundant, "took their meals" and then "partook of food," in order to cover up what the Bible really says.

But these are not unintentional mistakes because the *New World Translation* does the same thing in Acts 20 when the breaking of bread is mentioned once again. This time it is on the first day of the week—the daily observance having now become (customarily) weekly. In the King James Version of the Bible Acts 20:7 and 11 read,

> And upon the first day of the week, when the disciples came together *to break bread*, Paul preached unto them. . . . When he, therefore, was come up again, and *had broken bread*, and eaten, and talked a long while, even till break of day, so he departed.

Now note how these verses have been translated in the NWT.

> On the first day of the week, when we were gathered together *to have a meal*, Paul began discoursing to them. . . . He now went upstairs and *began the meal* and took food, and after conversing for quite a while, until daybreak, he at length departed.

Once again there are footnotes after "meal" in both verses 7 and 11 that read, "to break bread" and "having broken the bread." Again I ask, why did the authors of the NWT use an entirely different wording and make it "meal" in the text and not the proper rendering of "to break bread"? Was it in order that readers of the NWT would not realize that the Memorial was observed on "the first day of the week"?

It is worth mentioning here that most people know the New Testament was originally written in Greek. The Watchtower Society printed its own modern Greek Bible. The phrase used for "breaking of bread" in the Greek manuscripts of the Bible is commonly used in the Greek language today. However, the Greek Bible published by the Society changed the words for breaking of bread from the original text to an entirely different wording to conform with its English translation. Not only has the Watchtower Society twisted its English *New World Translation*, it has also corrupted its Greek *New World Translation*.

If the Watchtower Society will go to such lengths to change the Bible in order to obscure when and how often the Memorial should be observed, can it be trusted not to change other Bible texts that may contradict its other practices and doctrines?

The Forbidding of Blood Transfusions

One of the most controversial and objectionable teachings of the Watchtower Society is the forbidding of its followers to receive blood transfusions. This was first instituted in 1945, though it didn't become a disfellowshipping policy until 1961. (Witnesses often say it is up to your conscience, but your conscience will surely tell you to go along with the society's teaching lest you be disfellowshipped.) Since a good percentage of the Witnesses blindly follow this unbiblical teaching, hundreds of thousands of them have died unnecessarily. Many of these have been children who were not allowed to choose for themselves. But many Witnesses who go along with this policy privately question if the Bible really does forbid blood transfusions and wonder if all these deaths could have been prevented.

Of course, the Bible says nothing about blood transfusions since this is a relatively new medical procedure that has saved untold millions of lives. Moreover, when the taking of blood is forbidden in the Bible, it always has to do with the "eating of blood." Eating is for nutrition. Receiving a blood transfusion is not for nutrition; the infusion goes directly into the bloodstream and begins its lifesaving work immediately.

The society quotes the words "You must not eat the blood of any sort of flesh," found in Leviticus 17:14, as proof for its unbiblical teaching against blood transfusions. Not only that, the society uses the statement at the end of the verse— "Anyone eating it will be cut off"—as justification for disfellowshipping anyone who receives a blood transfusion and defies the dictates of the Watchtower Society.

But is this what the Bible actually teaches? Those who lived in biblical times knew nothing about blood transfusions, so this dictate surely didn't suggest a blood transfusion to them. What does it mean? The Jews then—and still today—apply this to the way animals are to be slaughtered, so that all the blood is drained out of the meat. It is then considered "kosher."

It is interesting to note that verses forbidding the eating of blood also prohibit the eating of fat. Leviticus 3:17 declares: "You must not eat any fat or any blood at all." In Leviticus 7:23–26 we read that both those who "eat blood" and those who "eat fat" "must be cut off." According to the Watchtower Society, this means "disfellowshipping." The society should be consistent and also disfellowship Jehovah's Witnesses who freely eat fat.

But very few Witnesses, let alone those people who are not Witnesses, are aware of the *initial argument* that the society put forth for forbidding blood transfusions, nor are they aware of the several changes that have taken place.

There used to be groups of people who believed that the human personality literally dwelt in the physical heart. For a while, the Watchtower Society accepted this theory. They felt that since the center of emotions and one's personality was in the physical heart, it was only logical that one's personality flowed through the bloodstream. Thus, when the society first prohibited blood transfusions, it felt that one's personality would be transferred to someone else and this was not right.

When AIDS came along, the society had a heyday and shifted its reason for forbidding blood transfusions. While we all decry the transferring of the AIDS virus due to blood transfusions, this doesn't make blood transfusions wrong. Now, however, as a result of improved testing procedures, the chance of contracting AIDS this way is slim, so the society's second argument has had to be laid aside.

As stated before, the society has drastically changed its stance on blood transfusions. It used to forbid *all* blood, but now about half of blood *components* or blood *products* can be received.

In order to help clear up some of this confusion, the Watchtower Society has set up Hospital Liaison Committees in most areas to study the situation and help Witness patients in the hospital understand what is permissible and what is not. But as people on these committees have studied the situation and realized the drastic changes in policy that have been made concerning the use of blood, they see many contradictions that can't be justified. Some of these people have quietly resigned while others, remaining anonymous, have voiced their opposition to the society policy toward blood transfusions via the Internet. They seem earnestly interested in making changes to this inappropriate ban.

I heard of a Jehovah's Witness with three children who at the age of forty-five died as a result of hepatitis C because he refused a blood transfusion. At the time, the family felt this was the right thing to do. But since then the wife has been exposed to Watchtower literature that reveals the many changes in the society's teachings and practices. She has now lost her confidence in the Watchtower and says, "My husband died in vain."

Chapter Nine

Analysis of Some Key Doctrines and Dates

Probably the widest difference between the Watchtower Society and Bible-believing churches (which the society refers to as "Christendom") involves teachings surrounding the nature of God and the timing of Christ's return. Let's take a look at some of these key doctrines, how the beliefs of the Jehovah's Witnesses differ from that of the historic Christian faith, and whose teaching is most faithful to Scripture.

The Trinity: A "Pagan" Doctrine?

One of the major goals of the Watchtower Society is to destroy confidence in any belief in the Trinity; that is, one God manifest in three persons: Father, Son and Holy Spirit. Whenever Jehovah's Witnesses are having a so-called "Bible study" with someone in his or her home, they usually don't get too far into their indoctrination course before they start calling the Trinity a "pagan" doctrine. The society describes the Trinity as a "three-headed pagan monster" and has gone to great lengths to portray the Trinity as a false teaching. To do this, the Watchtower has distorted the true teaching of the Trinity beyond all recognition and is actually attacking a caricature of the doctrine, not what Trinitarians really believe.

The society also has a corrupt way of trying to disprove the biblical teaching of the Trinity. The Watchtower's 32-page booklet entitled *Should You Believe in the Trinity?* has over a hundred quotes from various encyclopedias and books. The only trouble is that all but one of these quotes is *out of context*, conveying the opposite of the original article's intended meaning. If the teaching of the Trinity is so "pagan," why does the society have to distort the writings of Trintarians to "prove" its point? On page 6 of this booklet, we read:

> *The New Encyclopaedia Britannica* observes: "Neither the word Trinity nor the explicit doctrine appears in the New Testament."

But what does the article *in context* actually say? It is found in volume 11, and reads thus:

> Neither the word Trinity nor the explicit doctrine appears in the New Testament, nor did Jesus and his followers intend to contradict the Shema in the Old Testament: "Hear, O Israel: The Lord our God is one Lord" (Deut. 6:4). The earliest Christians, however, had to cope with the implications of the coming of Jesus Christ and of the presumed presence of the power of God among them—i.e., the Holy Spirit, whose coming was connected with the celebration of [the feast of] Pentecost. The Father, Son, and Holy Spirit were associated in such New Testament passages as the Great Commission: "Go therefore and make disciples of all nations, baptizing them in the name of the Father and of the Son and of the Holy Spirit" (Matt. 28:19); and in the apostolic benediction: "The grace of the Lord Jesus Christ and the love of God

and the fellowship of the Holy Spirit be with you all" (II Cor. 13:14). Thus the New Testament established the basis for the doctrine of the Trinity.

It is clear that if the society had quoted the article in context it would have supported the fact that the Trinity is a biblical teaching and not a "pagan" doctrine as it claims.

Another quote found on page 4 of the same booklet reads:

> This confusion is widespread. The *Encyclopedia Americana* notes that the doctrine of the Trinity is considered to be "beyond the grasp of human reason."

But what does the *Encyclopedia Americana* actually say in context?

> It is held that although the doctrine is beyond the grasp of human reason, it is, like many of the formulations of physical science, not contrary to reason, and may be apprehended (though it may not be comprehended) by the human mind.

> The theistic faith is completely taken for granted in the New Testament and in the early Christian creeds. Instead of reversion in the direction of polytheism, with a plurality of divine beings, the development of Trinitarian doctrine was guided by the same principle of divine revelation as that reflected in the Old Testament, that is, from plurality to unity. For the early Christian belief that Jesus was divine, the Son of God, and that as the risen, glorified Messiah, or Lord, He was now at the right hand of God, required the use of theistic language. . . . Prayer was addressed to the risen, glorified Christ. . . . Though at first impersonal (compare Acts 8:15–16, 10:44), as if the Spirit could be referred to as "it," in time the language of Christian preaching, teaching, and worship clearly involved the conception of a divine person. The Spirit from God, sent by God, was also divine, and therefore was God. Such formulas as Paul's "The grace of the Lord Jesus Christ and the love of God and the fellowship of the Holy Spirit" (II Corinthians 13:13) [make this clear].

How could an honest writer or editor quote from over a hundred sources and not get more than one of them correct? This must have been done deliberately, in order to deceive.

This attack on the Trinity is not limited to one book or article. Almost all Jehovah's Witnesses carry a copy of the Watchtower Society's publication *Reasoning from the Scriptures* in their briefcase. When asked a question to which they do not know the answer, they pull out this book and begin leafing through it to find what they want. Pages 405–26 of this book contains an article which quotes from five different sources to try to disprove the Trinity. Again, all five are mere partial quotes that give the opposite of the article's intended meaning.

The August 1, 1984, *Watchtower* has an article entitled "How Christendom Came to Worship an Unknown God." It cites six sources to try to portray the Trinity as a pagan doctrine, but once again all six are only partial quotes, conveying the opposite of what the author intended.

All one has to do is spend about thirty minutes in a public library to discover that the Watchtower's publications have greatly distorted the meaning of their quoted sources. While the society misquotes many articles, it has the audacity to include statements such as the following in its publications:

> Be very careful to be accurate in all statements you make. Use evidence honestly. In quotations, do not twist the meaning of a writer or speaker or use only partial quotations to give a different thought than the person intended. Also if you use statistics, use them properly. Statistics can often be used to give a distorted picture. (*Qualified to Be Ministers*, 1967, p. 199)

> Accuracy of statement. Jehovah's Witnesses are an organization of truth. We should want to speak the truth and be absolutely accu-

rate in every detail at all times. This should be so not only as regards doctrine but also in our quotations, what we say about others or how we represent them. (*Theocratic Ministry School Guidebook*, 1971, p. 110)

Anyone who has read even a small number of Watchtower publications will soon notice that they hardly ever quote anything in complete context. Their constant use of elliptical marks (. . .) to indicate omissions in the text is a tell-tale sign. Those who take the time to discover what is missing from the quoted material soon recognize how unreliable the Watchtower's writings really are. If the society was based on the truth, it would have no reason to distort the facts.

The biblical teaching of one God manifested in three persons, the Father, Son and Holy Spirit, is not a pagan teaching but a precious truth at the very heart of Christianity. Without it, there is no certainty for the future. With it, a person can be 100% sure of going to heaven the moment he dies because Christ shed His blood for our personal sins, which satisfied the holiness of the Father. The Holy Spirit is the one who sanctifies, seals and empowers the believer. The apostle Paul stated it so beautifully: "May the grace of the Lord Jesus Christ, and the love of God, and the fellowship of the Holy Spirit be with you all" (2 Cor. 13:14, NIV).

The word "Trinity" itself is not found in the Bible, but this hardly disproves anything. The basic teaching for the *doctrine* of the Trinity is found in the Bible. The Watchtower itself uses many words that are not in God's Word, like "Jehovah's Witnesses," "theocratic government," "Kingdom Hall," "governing body," etc.

While it is impossible to give a human example to illustrate the tri-unity of God, probably the best approximation is that of a family. Consider a husband, wife and son. They make up one family, but there are three persons in the family. Even though the functions of the three are different, they are equal. There is order in the family, but that does not mean superiority or inferiority. The Godhead is made up of three persons, but only one God. The functions of the Father, Son and Holy Spirit are different, but they are all of equal importance.

In the Bible the divine attributes ascribed to the Father are also ascribed to the Son and the Holy Spirit.

ATTRIBUTE	FATHER	SON	HOLY SPIRIT
Eternalness	Psalm 90:2	Rev. 1:8, 17	Heb. 9:14
Omnipotence	1 Pet. 1:5	2 Cor. 12:9	Rom. 15:19
Omniscience	Jer. 17:10	Rev. 2:23	1 Cor. 2:11
Omnipresence	Jer. 23:24	Matt. 18:20	Psalm 139:7
Holiness	Rev. 15:4	Acts 3:14	Luke 1:15
Truth	John 7:28	Rev. 3:7	1 John 5:6
Benevolence	Rom. 2:4	Eph. 5:25	Neh. 9:20
Communion	1 John 1:3	1 John 1:3	2 Cor. 13:14

God: Isn't He Omnipresent?

Most people, including Jehovah's Witnesses, are not aware that the god of the Watchtower Society is not omnipresent—that is, present everywhere. In fact, the god of the Watchtower Society is not able to do some things that angels can do. The society teaches that God is a "spirit," that He dwells in a "spirit body" and is confined to just one location. From 1891 to 1953 the society taught that God lived on the star Alcyone, which is part of the Pleiades constellation. In the Watchtower publication *Thy Kingdom Come* (*Studies in the Scriptures*), Volume III, 1891, of the 1903 edition, we read:

> It is now ascertained that the sun also is in motion, carrying with it its splendid retinue of comets, planets, its satellites and theirs, around some other and vastly mightier center. Astronomers are not yet fully agreed as to what or where that center is. Some, however, believe that they have found the direction of it to be the Pleiades, and particularly Alcyone, the central one of the renowned Pleiadic stars. To the distinguished German astronomer, Prof. J.H. Maedler, belongs the honor of having made this discovery. Alcyone, then, as far as science has been able to perceive, would seem to be "the midnight throne" in which the whole system of gravitation has its central seat, and from which the Almighty governs his universe.

Then in the book *Reconciliation*, 1928, on page 14 we read:

> The constellation of the seven stars forming the Pleiades appears to be the crowning center around which the known systems of the planets revolve even as our sun's planets obey the sun and travel in their respective orbits. It has been suggested, and with much weight, that one of the stars of that group is the dwelling-place of Jehovah and the place of the highest heavens; that it is the place to which the inspired writer referred when he said: "Hear thou from thy dwelling-place, even from heaven" (II Chron. 6:21); and that it is the place to which Job referred when under inspiration he wrote: "Canst thou bind the sweet influences of Pleiades, or loose the bands of Orion?"—Job 38:31.

> The constellation of Pleiades is a small one compared with others which scientific instruments disclose to the wondering eyes of man. But the greatness in size of other stars or planets is small when compared with the Pleiades in importance, because Pleiades is the place of the eternal throne of God.

The Watchtower Society claims that it can prove everything it teaches from the Bible. You will note that it even quotes a Bible verse to try to prove its point. However, the advancement in science seems to have proven to the Watchtower Society that Pleiades is no longer the center of the universe, as had been claimed for many years. In 1953 the society abandoned the idea of trying to identify the exact location where God now dwells. In the November 15, 1953, *Watchtower*, under the section "Questions from Readers" answering a question about Job 38:31–32 we find:

> Pleiades can no longer be considered the center of the universe and it would be unwise for us to try to fix God's throne as being at a particular spot in the universe. Were we to think of the Pleiades as his throne we might improperly view with special veneration that cluster of stars.

Note that the society said, "It would be unwise for us to try to fix God's throne at a particular spot in the universe." Since this is what the society did for over sixty years, wasn't it "unwise" for quite a long time? But even though the society *now* does not try to identify exactly where God lives, it has not abandoned the idea that God is still confined to one specific location. In the 1982 book *You Can Live Forever in Paradise on Earth*, we read: "Since God is a person with a spiritual body, he must have a place to live. The Bible tells us that the heavens are God's 'established *place* of dwelling.' (1 Kings 8:43)" [the italics are in the original text].

Since the society teaches that God is confined to one location and does not move about in the universe, then God is limited. Thus, the god of the Watchtower Society is not omnipresent, as Solomon describes in 2 Chronicles 6:18(NWT) where we read: "But will God truly dwell with mankind upon the earth? Look! Heaven, yes, the heaven of the heavens themselves, cannot contain you; how much less, then, this house that I have built?"

The Watchtower teaches that angels are "spirits" who live in "spirit bodies," which is how they describe God. However, angels are able to freely commute between heaven and earth and don't seem to be confined to just one location. In fact, the society teaches that evil angels came to this earth in the days of Noah and took upon themselves bodies, became men, married and had children. Yet it confines God to one place and denies that the Son of God could come down from heaven and dwell here bodily as the Lord Jesus Christ.

The only way that the god of the Watchtower Society knows what is going on in the universe and on this earth is for the angels to travel around gathering information and going back to his dwelling place and telling him. Also, their god has to communicate through angels if he wants any information to be transmitted to earth.

I have never seen any official Watchtower statement as to how God communicates with the men on the governing body, but I have heard that what takes place in the council of God is passed on to the Son (who is Michael, an archangel, according to the society) and then the Son passes it on to angels, who in turn pass it on to the men on the governing body. In the January 1, 1998, *Watchtower* there is a bold claim that the Watchtower Society is "under angelic guidance." However, I have not been given a sufficient answer as to how the society could make so many mistakes (such as setting the wrong date for the end of the world *five times*) if it is really receiving messages from God through angels and is "under angelic guidance"!

The Pronunciation of God's Names

The Watchtower Society distributes a 32-page pamphlet titled *THE DIVINE NAME That Will Endure Forever.* It comments on the words from Matthew 6:9, "Hallowed be your name," and claims that the only way God's name can be hallowed is by calling God "Jehovah." It declares that this name was once in the Bible but man has taken it out.

In reality, God's name has never been removed from the Bible. Obviously it is still there in the original Hebrew. What the society actually means is that the Hebrew word used by God to distinguish Himself from others is not found in most translations of the Bible.

However, an *equivalent* word for God's name *is* to be found in *all* Bible translations. In English, we use the word "LORD" (all letters in capitals) to indicate God's name—which is equivalent to the Hebrew YHWH. So the name of God has *not* been taken out of our Bible.

Furthermore, we are nowhere commanded by God to use His name in Hebrew only. The Watchtower Society is deceitful when it says that in most Bibles God's name has been removed. God's name has *not* been taken out of any Bible.

It was in order to emphasize God's name that Rutherford changed the name of the society from "Bible Students" to "Jehovah's Witnesses" in 1931. However, "Jehovah" is a false rendering of the Hebrew name for God, a fact that can be verified in just about every dictionary or encyclopedia. For instance:

- *WEBSTER'S COLLEGIATE DICTIONARY.* "Jehovah is a false rendering of the Hebrew YAHWEH."

- *ENCYCLOPEDIA AMERICANA.* "Jehovah is an erroneous form of the name of the God of Israel."

- *THE JEWISH ENCYCLOPEDIA.* "Jehovah is a mispronunciation of the Hebrew YHWH, the name of God."

- *MERIT'S STUDENT ENCYCLOPEDIA.* "Jehovah is an inaccurate reconstruction of the name of God in the Old Testament."

- *ENCYCLOPEDIA JUDAICA*, VOL. 7. "YHWH. The personal name of the God of Israel is written in the Hebrew Bible with the four consonants YHWH and is referred to as the 'Tetragrammation.' At least until the destruction of the First Temple in 586 B.C.E. this name was regularly pronounced with its proper vowels, as is clear from the Lachish Letters, written shortly before that date. . . . When Christian scholars of Europe first began to study Hebrew, they did not understand what this really meant, and they introduced the hybrid name 'Jehovah.' . . . The true pronunciation of the name YHWH was never lost. Several early Greek writers of the Christian Church testify that the name was pronounced 'Yahweh.' This is confirmed, at least for the vowel of the first syllable of the name, by the shorter form Jah." (See Exodus 15:2 and Psalm 68:4 in the *New World Translation*.)

If it is so important to use the Hebrew word for God's name instead of the English word "LORD," the Watchtower Society should at least use the *proper* pronunciation—which is YAHWEH. Most scholars agree that this is the closest to the correct pronunciation. (The fact that most scholars agree that the most accurate name for God in Hebrew is YAHWEH is acknowledged in the Spanish edition of the August 8, 1998, *Awake*.) The Jehovah's Witnesses often say, "When we make a mistake, we admit it and correct it." But for over sixty years it has been using a false rendering for the name of God with no sign of admitting this mistake to the English-speaking world or making any change.

Is the Society More Important than Jesus?

Jesus Christ is central to Christianity. True Christians are followers of Jesus Christ. But to Jehovah's Witnesses, Jesus Christ is not central; they continually talk about "Jehovah." I have talked to a number of Witnesses who become quite upset when I frequently refer to Jesus Christ. But while they emphasize "Jehovah," the New Testament puts the emphasis on Jesus Christ. In the Watchtower's *New World Translation* of the New Testament, it has inserted the name Jehovah 237 times where we typically would see the word "Lord." It disregards completely the fact that the name "Jesus Christ" is mentioned 912 times in the New Testament.

The Watchtower Society uses a few overworked verses to try to disprove the fact that Jesus Christ is equal with the Father.

Jehovah's Witnesses are very cautious in what they say about Jesus. They teach that Jesus was "only a man" while on earth, and existed as the archangel Michael in heaven before He came to earth. But when Witnesses are pressed as to *how* Michael came down and became Jesus, they have no answer. If the Watchtower Society ever admitted that any of the personality, will, mind or "something" that existed in heaven had come down and dwelt in Jesus Christ, then Jesus would have to be more than just a man, but they are not willing to accept this.

The society teaches that Jesus Christ died only for our past sins. Witnesses may *say* that He is their Savior or Redeemer, but beware! By this they mean that He saves us only from those sins we inherited in Adam at birth, and *not* our personal sins. Their emphasis is on one's faithfulness to "Jehovah's Organization"—the Watchtower Society. Jehovah's

Witnesses will say they believe in Jesus and that He is very important to them, but this does not mean He is important for their *salvation*. It means Jesus, as King (really Michael the archangel) during the Millennium, is very important to their teachings.

We find written in the Watchtower's book *Reasoning from the Scriptures* this quotation: "His perfect life given in sacrifice makes it possible for us to have forgiveness of sins. But I know that it is also vital to pay attention to his instructions regarding our responsibility as Christians." While this statement may sound nice, what it means is that Jesus merely opened a door so that we might strive to enter into eternal life. Jehovah's Witnesses must be 100% in submission to the Watchtower at all times, no matter how much the organization keeps changing its teachings. The November 15, 1981, *Watchtower* invites people to come to Jehovah's organization for salvation. It teaches that there is no salvation outside of the Watchtower.

But in stark contrast to the Watchtower Society's teaching, the Bible teaches that we are to come to *Jesus Christ* for salvation. Jesus said in Matthew 11:28, "Come unto me, all ye that labor and are heavy laden, and I will give you rest" (KJV). Jesus offers people salvation right now through His precious blood that He shed for our personal sins.

Considering the low esteem they place on the person of Jesus Christ, it is not surprising that the Watchtower Society also does not believe in His bodily resurrection from the grave. Using very deceptive wording concerning the resurrection, the society teaches that Christ was "only a man" whose body disintegrated into gases when He died, never to be seen again.

However, in an interesting bit of double talk, the society also states, "Jesus died at 33 1/2 years of age. But on the third day after his death he was resurrected to life. Forty days later he returned to heaven. (Acts 1:3, 9–11) There, as a spirit person once more he appeared 'before the person of God for us,' carrying the value of his ransom sacrifice" (*You Can Live Forever in Paradise on Earth,* p. 62).

How can the Watchtower say that Christ rose from the dead if His body decomposed into gases? How can it say He rose as "a spirit person" when it also teaches that "the spirit" is only breath that keeps a person alive? Furthermore, the society teaches that man does not have a soul—or anything that has personality—which can think, speak, hear or exist without the body. If the body of Jesus putrefied to gases, never to be seen again, what was left to be raised?

But the Bible clearly states over one hundred times that Christ rose bodily from the grave. The Bible never speaks about Jesus Christ being raised as "a spirit." Luke 24:37 tells us the disciples' reaction at seeing Jesus. "They were terrified and affrighted, and supposed that they had seen a spirit." Luke 24:38–39 tells us what Jesus said: "Why are ye troubled? and why do thoughts arise in your hearts? Behold my hands and my feet, that it is I myself: handle me, and see; for a spirit hath not flesh and bones, as ye see me have." Yet in spite of this clear Scripture passage, the Watchtower continues to speak of the resurrection of Jesus as something "spiritual" and not "literal."

After questioning Jehovah's Witnesses for eight years, I found out what the society actually believes happened when Jesus was born on earth. The society claims Michael the Archangel willed himself out of existence in heaven. How he did that no one knows. But it further teaches that after Jesus Christ died and was changed into gases, on the third day the Father re-created Michael and sent him to earth.

The spirit Michael, according to the Watchtower, went around appearing to the disciples and others in a body, saying that he was really the resurrected man, Jesus Christ, and after forty days returned to heaven. This would have been a very deceptive impersonation. The society often calls this Michael "Jesus Christ." Why it does this when the society has already said Jesus died and returned to gases is hard to understand.

Is the Holy Spirit Only "an Active Force"?

The Watchtower Society teaches that the Holy Spirit is "God's active force"—that He is not a person and does not have a personality. To try to prove their teachings, the society gives the following explanation in their book *INSIGHT on the Scriptures*, Volume 2:

> Lacks personal identification. Since God himself is a Spirit and is holy and since all his faithful angelic sons are spirits and are holy, it is evident that if the 'holy spirit' were a person, there should reasonably be given some means in the Scriptures to distinguish and identify such spirit person from all these other 'holy spirits.' It would be expected that, at the very least, the definite article would be used with it in all cases where it is not called 'God's holy spirit' or is not modified by some similar expression. This would at least distinguish it as THE Holy Spirit. But, on the contrary, in a large number of cases the expression 'holy spirit' appears in the original Greek without the article, thus indicating its lack of personality.

The article goes on to give twenty-one verses in the New Testament where the definite article "the" is not found when the Holy Spirit is referred to. But in the Watchtower's *own translation* of the Bible, I easily found *108* places where the definite article "the" *is* found in connection with the Holy Spirit—*five times* as many verses! The Spirit of God *did* distinguish Himself as "THE Holy Spirit." Any honest editor would check out the facts before writing such a distorted statement.

In the society's book *You Can Live Forever in Paradise on Earth*, which Jehovah's Witnesses used from 1982 to 1995 in proselytizing inquirers, we read the following statement under the section "God—Who is He?" "By means of his holy spirit God created the heavens, the earth and all living things." I have asked many Jehovah's Witnesses to explain to me how an "impersonal force" can create. I have never received an answer. I continued by asking them how God can instruct an "impersonal force" in order to give it wisdom to create? Again I received no answer. I *received* no answer because there *is* no answer. Impersonal material cannot create. Only a person with almighty power and knowledge could create this universe.

I think it is much easier to believe the Bible, where the Holy Spirit is proven to be a person. Many Scripture passages clearly demonstrate that the Holy Spirit must be a person.

- *How could an impersonal force speak?* The Bible teaches that the Holy Spirit spoke definite messages to men upon this earth. A few references are found in: Acts 8:29; 13:2; 20:23; 28:25; 1 Tim. 4:1; Heb. 9:8; Rev. 2:7, 11, 17, 29; 3:6, 13, 22; 14:13; 22:17.

- *How could something that is not a person be grieved?* Ephesians 4:30 warns us not to "grieve the Holy Spirit."

- *How could a sin so great that it is unforgivable be a sin against an inactive force?* In Matthew 12:31–32 Jesus mentions the sin of blasphemy against the Holy Spirit which can't be forgiven.

- *How is it possible for humans to have "fellowship" with an inanimate object or force?* Second Corinthians 13:14 speaks about "the fellowship of the Holy Spirit." The Holy Spirit has to be a person in order for us to have fellowship with Him.

1874 or 1914—Which?

For years the date 1914 has been at the very center of Watchtower theology. In 1914, the society teaches, Christ began His 1000-year reign in heaven. To the Jehovah's Witnesses, it was a sign that this old world system would end very soon and the creation of the new earth would begin. At the present time the entire truthfulness of the society's teachings stands upon this 1914 date. But upon investigation this date will not stand up to the society's claims.

Very few Jehovah's Witnesses today are aware that for over fifty years the Watchtower used 1874, not 1914, as the date when Christ began to reign in heaven (1914 was predicted as the starting date for the battle of Armageddon, which would usher in the new world). The following quotes from Watchtower publications show that for many years 1874 was taught as the date that Christ's heavenly reign began.

- *Studies in the Scriptures* (1888), Vol. 2, p. 239: "Christ's presence and the harvest began in 1874."

- *Studies in the Scriptures* (1897), Vol. 4, p. 621: "Our Lord, the appointed King, is now present, since October 1874 . . . and the formal inauguration of his kingly office dates from April 1878."

- *Studies in the Scriptures* (1917), Vol. 7, p. 68: "Scriptures prove that the Lord's Second Advent was in 1874."

- *The Watchtower,* Mar. 1, 1923, p. 67: "The Scriptures show that the second presence [of the Lord] was due in 1874. . . . This proof shows that the Lord has been present since 1874."

- *The Watchtower*, Jan. 1, 1924, p. 5: "Surely there is not the slightest room for doubt in the mind of a truly consecrated child of God that the Lord Jesus is present and has been since 1874."

- *Creation* (1927), p. 289: "The second coming of the Lord therefore began in 1874."

- *Prophecy* (1929), p. 65: "The Scriptural proof is that the second presence of the Lord Jesus Christ began in 1874."

When the 1874 date was presented as the time Christ began to reign in heaven, it was not presented as a "theory" or "speculation" but as a date clearly shown in the Bible. Did God make a mistake? Of course not; the Watchtower Society's leaders made a mistake. However, it was not until 1930, sixteen years after Christ was supposed to have begun to reign in 1914, that an announcement was made by the Watchtower leaders that the date had been changed from 1874 to 1914. And even then, it was not made official until 1943.

Chapter Ten

The *New World Translation* of the Bible

The Watchtower Society tries to give the impression that its *New World Translation* of the Bible is scholarly and accurate. But in the light of evidence to the contrary, can this claim be substantiated?

Work on the *New World Translation* began in 1946. It was published in six volumes, released from 1950 to 1960, beginning with the New Testament, which the Society refers to as the "Christian Greek Scriptures," and then the Old Testament, referred to as the "Hebrew Scriptures." The first complete Bible was copyrighted in 1961 and revised in 1981 and 1984. But in the true sense of the word, it is not a translation because it was not actually translated from the Hebrew and Greek at all.

Not a Scholarly Translation

The "Bethelites" (workers at the Watchtower's Brooklyn

headquarters) were some of the people who worked on the *New World Translation*, but they had no linguistic skills or education in foreign languages when they entered Bethel. Most of those who go to the Brooklyn headquarters do so at the age of eighteen, with only a high school education at best.

The only exception to this was Frederick Franz, who attended college for three years and studied some Greek during that time. Two or three years of college Greek, however, hardly qualifies a person to be a "Greek scholar." Even more significant is the fact that he only studied Greek and not Hebrew.

There is no evidence that the Watchtower Society's translation committee ever requested the help of any recognized Greek or Hebrew scholars. There is no evidence that any of them even knew any Greek or Hebrew, except for the little that Franz knew. One could argue that perhaps they educated themselves in Greek and Hebrew—but there is no evidence for that supposition either.

Even if they did, I certainly wouldn't want to put my physical body into the care of a "self-educated" doctor, especially when there are so many properly educated ones available. Why then should I place my faith in the hands of a translation of the Bible—which may determine my eternal destiny—compiled by a group of "self-educated" translators, especially when there are so may accurate translations of the Bible—by recognized Hebrew and Greek scholars—to choose from?

The *New World Translation* is really not a translation taken directly from the original Greek and Hebrew but a compilation of material taken from about twenty-five other English translations of the Bible. It seems obvious that the men on the committee searched multitudes of English Bible translations to find verses that seemed to agree with their interpretation instead of going directly to the Greek and Hebrew. If you read any of the Watchtower material, you will recognize that they often quote from rather obscure translations, especially from those by a single translator, in order to find verses that agree with them.

Examples include the only two translations of the Bible I know of which translate the end of John 1:1 as "a god," as the NWT renders it. One is *The New Testament in An Improved Version*, published in London, England, in 1808, and based upon a text written by a Unitarian. The other version that translates John 1:1 as "a god" was conducted by Johannes Greber.

In both the September 15, 1962, *Watchtower*, under a discussion as to why the NWT translated John 1:1 as "a god," and in the booklet *"The Word"—Who Is He? According to John*, we find the same footnote which reads:

> *The New Testament—A New Translation and Explanation* Based on the Oldest Manuscripts, by Johannes Greber (a translation from German into English), edition of 1937, the front cover of this bound translation being stamped with a golden cross.

Who was Johannes Greber? He was a former Roman Catholic priest who became a "spiritist"—one who communicates with the spirit world. His wife was a "medium" who also helped Greber in his translation of the New Testament. But while the Watchtower Society condemns "spiritism," it still used Johannas Greber's translation "as a reliable translation" when it knew Greber's background.

In the February 15, 1956, *Watchtower*, there is an article entitled "Triumphing Over Wicked Spirit Forces." This is an article that decries spiritism and uses Johannes Greber as an example of a spiritist and the kind of people who should be avoided. Let me quote from this article:

> Says Johannes Greber in the introduction of his translation of the New Testament, copyrighted in 1937: 'I myself was a Catholic priest, and until I was forty-eight years old had never as much as believed in the possibility of communicating with the world of God's spirits. The day came, however, when I involuntarily took my first step toward such communication, and experienced things that shook me to the depths of my soul. . . . My experiences are related in a book that has appeared in both German and English and bears the title, *Communication with the Spirit-World: Its Laws and Its Purposes*.' (Page 15, ¶, 2, 3) In keeping with his Roman Catholic extraction Greber's translation is bound with a gold-leaf cross on its stiff front cover. In the Foreword of his aforementioned book ex-priest Greber says: 'The most significant spiritualistic book is the Bible.' Under this impression Greber endeavors to make his New Testament translation read very spiritualistic.
>
> Very plainly the spirits in which ex-priest Greber believes helped him in his translation.

You will note that the Watchtower Society knew in 1956 that Greber was a spiritist and they condemned him for this. Yet six years later it used his translation as one of its two sources for translating John 1:1 as "a god." Greber did not even believe in the inspiration of the New Testament. Yet the Watchtower Society still cited Greber in their 1971 publication *Aid to Bible Understanding*, and in the October 15, 1975, *Watchtower*, as a source for their rendering of Matthew 27:52.

But after it became widely known that the Watchtower Society used a spiritist like Greber as proof for their accuracy in the translation of John 1:1 and Matthew 27:52, the society conveniently decided to cease using him. In the April 1, 1983, *Watchtower*, under the section "Questions from Readers," we find the question: "Why, in recent years, has *The Watchtower* not made use of the translation by the former Catholic priest, Johannes Greber?" Here is their answer:

> This translation was used occasionally in support of renderings of Matthew 27:52, 53 and John 1:1, as given in the *New World Translation* and other authoritative Bible versions. But as indicated in a foreword to the 1980 edition of *The New Testament* by Johannes Greber, this translator relied on "God's Spirit World" to clarify for him how he should translate difficult passages. It is stated: "His wife, a medium of God's spirit world, was often instrumental in conveying the correct answers from God's Messengers to Pastor Greber." *The Watchtower* has deemed it improper to make use of a translation that has such a close rapport with spiritism. (Deuteronomy 18:10–12) The scholarship that forms the basis for the rendering of the above-cited texts in the *New World Translation* is sound and for this reason does not depend at all on Greber's translation for authority. Nothing is lost, therefore, by ceasing to use his *New Testament*.

Notice that the society tried to suggest that it had *just found out* about Greber being a spiritist from the 1980 edition, when in reality it already knew in 1956 from his 1937 publication that he was a spiritist. This goes to show that the Watchtower Society will go to any length to try to find a source that seems to prove its own predetermined individual interpretation of certain Bible verses.

But this is not the end of the story. The Watchtower Society has produced quite an extensive index of all the articles it has produced in its books and magazines, with the subjects covered and Scripture verses used. In the *Watch Tower Publications Index 1930–1985,* Johannes Greber is mentioned:

GREBER, JOHANNES
The New Testament by:
close rapport with spiritism: w83 4/1 31
John 1:1:   w62 554

This index, however, fails to mention the lengthy article in the February 15, 1956, *Watchtower*, where it clearly states that it knew that Greber was a spiritist. Why did it purposely leave out this reference? It also fails to mention at least six other references to Greber in its writings. (See *What Do the Scriptures Say About "Survival After Death"?*, *The Watchtower,* October 1, 1955, *Make Sure of All Things—Hold Fast to What Is Fine*, 1965, *Aid to Bible Understanding*, 1971, *The Watchtower*, October 15, 1975, and *The Watchtower*, April 15, 1976.)

But this is still not the end of the story. The Watchtower Society claims that all Jehovah's Witnesses around the world read the same material. This is not true. The "Questions from Readers" (which are really questions posed by the editors of the magazine) that mentions they do not refer to Greber anymore, was *not* printed in the Spanish *Watchtower*. Therefore, those who read the Spanish edition did not know that all references to Greber had been dropped. When the Watchtower Society translated and published the book *Aid to Bible Understanding* (*Ayuda para Entender la Biblia*) in Spanish in 1987, it still used Johannes Greber as its source for translating John 1:1 as "a god." Wouldn't this be considered planned deception?

The Watchtower Society has translated the entire Bible into thirty-three foreign languages and the New Testament into nineteen other languages as of 2005. Since a number of things that I had found while examining the English *New*

World Translation agreed exactly with the *New World Translation* in other languages, I came to the conclusion that all of the *New World Translations* of the Bible into other languages had been made from the English and not from Greek and Hebrew. Then, to my surprise, in the October 15, 1997, *Watchtower,* the society came out and admitted that all of the *New World Translations* into other languages were taken from the English *New World Translation* (which itself is not a translation from the original Greek and Hebrew but a compilation from many English versions). The article tries to justify this position:

> Translating from the English, rather than working directly from the Hebrew and Greek, offers important advantages. Besides shortening translation time, it makes possible greater unity of expression in all languages. Why? Because it is much easier to translate precisely from one modern language into another than to translate from an ancient language into various modern ones. After all, translators can consult with native speakers of modern languages but not of languages spoken thousands of years ago.

Is speed and "unity of expression" the most important things to look for in translating the Bible? Shouldn't we be more interested in *accuracy*? Besides, although the society says it is interested in speed, apparently it isn't *that* interested, because it has produced the whole Bible in only seventeen languages since 1963, while producing its own Watchtower publications in over a hundred languages. This seems to indicate that Watchtower literature is considered more important than the Bible itself!

Second, why would translating from only one language, English, provide more "unity of expression" than translating from the one original language—Hebrew for the Old Testament and Greek for the New Testament? This would be working with only one language for each Testament.

Third, even though Hebrew is an ancient language, it is spoken, read and understood by millions of Jews today. Did the Watchtower Society forget that? It would be very easy to find people who know biblical Hebrew. And even though the vernacular Greek used in the Scriptures is not exactly the same language as modern Greek, much of the vocabulary is still the same. Students all around the world study the Greek that the New Testament was written in. It would be easy to find people who could translate from the Greek.

A translation from the original language is much more accurate than a translation taken from an English translation. One example from the *New World Translation* proves what I am trying to say. In the English version, Acts 21:20 reads:

> After hearing this they began to glorify God, and they said to him: "You behold, brother, how many thousands of believers there are among the Jews; and they are all zealous for the Law."

Here the *New World Translation* followed a number of English versions and used the word "thousands." In the original Greek text the word used here is "myriads" which means "ten thousands." This word "myriads" is still used by the Greeks today. But in the *New World Translation* of the modern Greek New Testament, instead of using the word "myriads" in this verse, which would be the proper rendering in Greek, it followed the English *New World Translation* and used the word for "thousands." This is an entirely different Greek word.

However, the *New World Translation* did use the word "myriads" in their Greek and English translations of the New

Testament in Hebrews 12:22, Jude 14 and Revelation 5:11. Why did the *New World Translation* use "myriads" in three places and then only "thousands" in one other place both in the English and other translations? This is especially confusing when we read what is written in the October 15, 1997, *Watchtower*:

> Secondly, consistency should be maintained, the translation holding to one rendering for each major word as far as the context reasonably permits. Such an approach helps readers to see how Bible writers used specific words.

Many more illustrations could be given where the society changed the text of the Bible to conform with its teaching, but these examples show that the *New World Translation* is not reliable in many important places.

Proves that Jesus Is "Jehovah"

The Bible ascribes the creation of the world to God (Genesis 1:1). The Bible goes more into detail and identifies the Creator as Jesus Christ. Since the Creator of the universe is God and Jesus Christ is the Creator, then it would seem obvious that Jesus Christ is truly God. But even though this truth is so clearly presented in the Bible, the Watchtower Society refuses to acknowledge it.

The society teaches that God the Father created the Son and *only* the Son. This Son it identifies not as Jesus Christ but as Michael the archangel, and it maintains that this Son (Michael) created everything else.

When the society says that Jesus is the Son of God, it does not believe that He is the Son who co-existed in heaven with the Father and came down to this earth, took upon

Himself human form, and was both God and man. The society does say that Jesus was conceived by the Holy Spirit, but even though it says this, it still teaches that Jesus was *only* a man and not divine. It does not believe that Jesus is the unique Son of God. It teaches that Jesus was "a son of God" in the exact same way as Adam was. Jesus thus can be identified as "a son of God" according to Watchtower theology, but He has no connection with the Son of God who existed in heaven.

The society states in its 1988 publication *INSIGHT on the Scriptures*, Volume 1: "This one, 'the firstborn of all creation,' was used by Jehovah in creating all other things, those in the heavens and those upon the earth, 'the things visible and the things invisible.'" The society uses Revelation 3:14 in the KJV which reads, "These things saith the Amen, the faithful and true witness, the beginning of the creation of God" to try to prove that the Son is a created being and greatly inferior to the Father. When one checks the word "beginning" (*arche*) in the Greek, he will find that it can also mean "origin" or "ruler." Hence it is translated in the NIV as "These are the words of the Amen, the faithful and true witness, the ruler of God's creation."

In order to hold to its unbiblical concept that there were two distinct acts of creation—(1) the Father creating the Son and (2) the Son creating everything else—the society has inserted the word "other" four times between "all" and "things" in Colossians 1:16–17 in its *New World Translation* of the Bible:

> Because by means of him all [other] things were created in the heavens and upon the earth, the things visible and the things invisible, no matter whether they are thrones or lordships or govern-

ments or authorities. All [other] things have been created through him and for him. Also, he is before all [other] things and by means of him all [other] things were made to exist.

Let us look at what the Bible has to say about the "Creator" and His identity. The beginning portion of John 1:1 is very important to this subject and puts a death blow to the Watchtower Society's teaching that the Son is a created being. Some literal translations of the first part of John 1:1 are "Originally was the Word" (Rotherham, 1897); "When the world began, the Word was already there" (Barclay, 1968); "When time began, the Word was there" (Kleist); "In the beginning of time the Word already was" (Sheed . . . Ward Press); "The Logos existed in the very beginning" (Moffatt); and "In the beginning the Word existed" (Williams, 1937). Since the first part of John 1:1 refers to the Creator (Logos, Word), who was already in existence when creation occurred, then the Creator (the Son, Jesus Christ) belonged to the order of eternity and cannot be a created being!

Colossians 1:16–17 is an important passage on this subject. When we leave out the added word "other" from the *New World Translation*, it reads:

> Because by means of him [the Son, identified in v. 13] all things were created in the heavens and upon the earth, the things visible and the things invisible, no matter whether they are thrones or lordships or governments or authorities. All things have been created through him and for him. Also, he is before all things and by means of him all things were made to exist.

These verses ascribe *all* creation to the Son; therefore it would be impossible for the Son to create Himself or be a created being.

John 1:3 says the same thing: "All things came into existence through him, and apart from him not even one thing came into existence" (NWT).

If what the Watchtower Society teaches is true—that the Father created the Son and then the Son created everything as God's representative—then John 1:3 would be proclaiming a lie. This verse says, "apart from him not even one thing came into existence." The society says that "one thing," "the Son," was created by the Father and then all other things were created by the Son. But this is not what the Bible teaches.

The first verse in the Bible, Genesis 1:1, should lay to rest forever the idea that Jesus Christ is not God. This verse is very familiar and reads: "In [the] beginning God created the heavens and the earth."

The Watchtower Society says that the Father created the Son and then the Son created everything else, which would include the heavens and the earth. But this verse says that it was "God" who "created the heavens and the earth" and not "a god."

Note carefully the following verses which state that it was Jehovah "Himself" who created the heavens and the earth. (All these verses are taken from the *New World Translation*.)

> You are worthy, Jehovah, even our God, to receive the glory and the honor and the power, because you created all things, and because of your will they existed and were created. (Rev. 4:11)

> This is the history of the heavens and the earth in the time of their being created, in the day that Jehovah God made earth and heaven. (Gen. 2:4)

> And Jehovah proceeded to answer Job out of the windstorm and say: . . . Where did you happen to be when I founded the earth?

Tell [me], if you do know understanding. Who set its measurements, in case you know, or who stretched out upon it the measuring line? Into what have its socket pedestals been sunk down, or who laid its cornerstone? (Job 38:1, 4-6)

By the word of Jehovah the heavens themselves were made, and by the spirit of his mouth all their army. (Ps. 33:6)

If you [Jehovah] send forth your spirit, they are created; and you make the face of the ground new. The glory of Jehovah will prove to be to time indefinite. Jehovah will rejoice in his works. (Ps. 104:30)

My help is from Jehovah, the Maker of heaven and earth. (Ps. 121:2)

This is what Jehovah has said, your Repurchaser and the Former of you from the belly: "I, Jehovah, am doing everything, stretching out the heavens by myself, laying out the earth. Who was with me?" (Isa. 44:24)

This is what Jehovah has said, the Holy One of Israel and the Former of him: "Ask me even about the things that are coming concerning my sons; and concerning the activity of my hands YOU people should command me. I myself have made the earth and have created even man upon it. I—my own hands have stretched out the heavens, and all the army of them I have commanded." (Isa. 45:11–12)

Moreover, my own hand laid the foundation of the earth, and my own right hand extended out the heavens. I am calling to them, that they may keep standing together. (Isa. 48:13)

Since Jesus Christ is the Creator and the Bible states over and over that Jehovah *Himself* (and not some delegated angel) is the Creator, then the Son, Jesus Christ, has to be Jehovah. The Watchtower Society can deny this truth, but the Bible teaches that Jehovah is the Creator of the heavens and the earth.

The *New World Translation* teaches in a second way that Jesus is Jehovah. In the Appendix of the 1984 Revised Large Reference edition of the *New World Translation*, we read: "The title '*A-dhohn*', 'Lord: Master,' when preceded by the definite article *ha*, 'the,' gives the expression *ha-'A-dhohn*', 'the [true] Lord.' The use of the definite article *ha* before the title '*A-dhohn*' limits the application of this title exclusively to Jehovah God."

Ha-A-dhohn is a Hebrew word. Translations of the Greek Scriptures have been made into Hebrew. The Watchtower Society is well aware of these translations. It uses them to determine where to place the Hebrew name for God, "Yahweh" (falsely rendered "Jehovah" by the Watchtower Society), in the Greek Scriptures of the *New World Translation*. When the Hebrew for God's name YHWH appears in these translations, the *New World Translation* uses the word "Jehovah." The Society has used the word "Jehovah" 237 times and slavishly followed these Hebrew translations.

As noted above, when the word *ha-A-dhohn* is used, it "limits the application of the title exclusively to Jehovah God." But there are at least 72 places where the word *ha-A-dhohn* is found in the Hebrew translations within the Greek Scriptures where, instead of saying "Jehovah" the *New World Translation* translates the word merely as "the Lord." Let us see what happens when we use the word "Jehovah" in place of "the Lord" as the Watchtower Society claims is appropriate. (All quotes are taken from the *New World Translation*.)

> Because there was born to YOU today a Savior, who is Christ *Jehovah*, in David's city. (Luke 2:11)

> Also, with great power the apostles continued giving forth the witness concerning the resurrection of *Jehovah* Jesus. (Acts 4:33)

So Ananias went off and entered into the house, and he laid his hands upon him and said: "Saul, brother, *Jehovah*, the Jesus that appeared to you on the road over which you were coming, has sent me forth, in order that you may recover sight and be filled with holy spirit." (Acts 9:17)

However, out of them there were some men of Cyprus and Cyrene that came to Antioch and began talking to the Greek-speaking people, declaring the good news of *Jehovah* Jesus. (Acts 11:20)

For I received from *Jehovah* that which I also handed on to YOU, that *Jehovah* Jesus in the night in which he was going to be handed over took a loaf. (1 Cor. 11:23)

Who killed even *Jehovah* Jesus and the prophets and persecuted us. (1 Thess. 2:15)

Because *Jehovah* himself will descend from heaven with a commanding call, with an archangel's voice and with God's trumpet, and those who are dead in union with Christ will rise first. Afterward we the living who are surviving will, together with them, be caught away in clouds to meet *Jehovah* in the air, and thus we shall always be with [the] Lord. (1 Thess. 4:16–17)

The Watchtower Society interprets this entire section of the epistle, verses 13–18, as a reference to the second coming of Christ Jesus. Since this passage says that "*Jehovah* himself" will return and it is Jesus Christ who will return, then the Bible teaches that Jesus is Jehovah. (There is a footnote in the NWT Reference Bible which acknowledges that in a number of translations "the Lord" means "Jehovah." So the one whom Christians meet in the air is not God the Father, but Jesus Christ, who is called Jehovah.)

Many other references could be given, but these should be enough proof that Jehovah is identified as the Lord Jesus Christ. The Watchtower Society has tried to conceal these facts and continues to deny the biblical position given to

Jesus Christ. The Holy Spirit, however, has put emphasis on "Jesus" because the only possible way that anyone can come to the Father is through the Lord Jesus Christ.

In John 14:6 we read, "Jesus said to him: 'I am the way and the truth and the life. No one comes to the Father except through me'" (NWT). Unless our sinful heart has been washed in the precious blood of the Lord Jesus Christ, we will never come into a personal relationship with the Father.

Jesus Christ did not die just to save us from the sins we inherited from Adam so that almost all people would be resurrected and given a second chance on the new earth to work for salvation. Jesus also died for our personal sins as the apostle Paul so aptly wrote in First Corinthians 15:3-4(NWT): "For I handed on to YOU, among the first things, that which I also received, that Christ died for *our* sin according to the Scriptures; and that he was buried, yes, that he has been raised up the third day according to the Scriptures."

Chapter Eleven

Important Conclusions

If you have read this far, a number of issues should be clear. When we consider the discrepancies between Watchtower teaching and the clear message of the Bible, we must come to some obvious conclusions.

It Is Biblical to Pray to Jesus

Once people have associated with the Jehovah's Witnesses for a period of time, they become quite confused as to how to pray and to whom to pray. The Witnesses continually approach God by using the title "Jehovah." But is this really biblical?

I would think that Jesus Christ should be the supreme example when it comes to prayer. We have a number of places in the Bible where Jesus prayed, and He always begins with the word "Father." (See, for example, Luke 22:42, 23:34, 46; John 17:1.) Never once does Jesus address His Father as "Jehovah." In fact, Jesus said in Matthew 6:9, "After this manner, therefore, pray ye: Our Father . . ." Thus, a biblical prayer will be addressed to the Father.

Also the Bible teaches that we can pray directly to Jesus. In Luke 23:42 the thief on the cross prayed to Jesus, and He answered the prayer. In Acts 7:59 Stephen prayed to Jesus Christ. The Bible does teach that it is all right to pray to Jesus.

You Should Check the Other Side

One of the things that the Watchtower Society (as well as many other religious groups) don't want you to do is to investigate their past. They will attack your religious beliefs and make false statements about them, but the Witnesses don't want you to question anything they say. However, is this not the very manner in which the Watchtower Society claims that people have been deceived about their present religion? It is much better to check them out before you enter in, because if you join without having all the facts, you may be sorry later. Truth does not mind being tested.

The Bible gives us a very clear warning of this in 1 John 4:1–3:

> Beloved ones, do not believe every inspired expression, but test the inspired expressions to see whether they originate with God, because many false prophets have gone forth into the world. You gain the knowledge of the inspired expression from God by this: Every inspired expression that confesses Jesus Christ as having come in the flesh originates with God, but every inspired expression that does not confess Jesus does not originate with God. Furthermore, this is the antichrist's [inspired expression] which YOU have heard was coming, and now it is already in the world. (NWT)

The Bible makes it clear that we are to test or prove all

religions, but Jehovah's Witnesses become quite upset when anyone tries to apply this to their organization. If you begin to ask them thought-provoking questions or bring up its past, they will accuse you of many things and drop you.

First John 5:1 shows that the Watchtower Society does not pass the test of being the true religion. It says: "Everyone believing that Jesus is the Christ has been born from God" (NWT).

If a person truly believes that Jesus is the Christ, then he will be born of God, or as we more commonly say, "born again." If you ask those of the "great crowd" of Jehovah's Witnesses if they have been born again, they will answer "No." Thus, they really do not believe that Jesus is the Christ, and they should be considered among the false teachers and prophets.

The Bible not only says that we are to test all religions, but we are told in Deuteronomy 13:14 to what degree we are to test them. This verse says: "You must also search and investigate and inquire thoroughly" (NWT).

A Japanese woman was becoming involved with the Jehovah's Witnesses. She was fairly complacent about the society's teachings, but she had a few questions. She talked to her husband about it. He was not opposed to the Jehovah's Witnesses, but since she had a few questions, he suggested she read a book on the subject. In this way she would know the truth.

She went to a Christian bookstore and bought my book *Approaching Jehovah's Witnesses in Love* in Japanese. She took it home and read it twice. That was enough to convince her that the Watchtower's teachings were not biblical. Not only that, she also sought out the church I started while a missionary in Japan (which I mentioned in the book). She began attending and in the process came to know Christ as her personal Savior, was baptized, and is now a church member.

I have a very dear friend who was the leading elder in his Kingdom Hall when I first met him. Over a period of years, he came to see the errors of the Watchtower Society and no longer attends their meetings. As we were talking one day, he said, "I was a Jehovah's Witness for twenty-nine years, but I was never satisfied."

I am acquainted with another Jehovah's Witness leader who is one of the saddest-looking men I know. He always has a long, sad face. At first I thought this was only my impression, but another man who knows him has also noticed his habitually morose countanence. If the elders are not satisfied and have no real joy in their lives, how can regular members expect to find any sense of joy and peace in their lives?

I know many people who have left the Watchtower Society. They all say that it was like a great, heavy burden or a dark cloud being lifted when they left.

There is absolutely nothing to lose by investigating a religious group; the Bible warns us that in the "latter days" many false teachers and prophets will arise. Truth can stand up to a thorough investigation.

If you do not investigate a religious group carefully before joining, you may have a lot to lose, however. False religions are easy to enter into but difficult to leave. And those who do have many deep scars the rest of their lives from the false teaching and the poor treatment they received.

Salvation Comes through Christ Alone, Not through Any Organization

The Watchtower Society teaches that God has always operated through an organization and that it is "God's sole channel of communication to this earth." In other words, the society claims to be *the only true organization* and salvation cannot be found outside of it. The following quotes make their belief on this subject quite clear.

> To get one's name written in that Book of Life will depend upon one's works. (*Watchtower*, April 1, 1947, p. 204)

> Put faith in a victorious organization! (*Watchtower*, March 1, 1979, p. 1)

> Those who desire life in the New Order must come into a right relationship with the organization. (*Watchtower*, November 15, 1981, pp. 16–17)

> . . . come to Jehovah's organization for salvation. . . . (*Watchtower*, November 15, 1981, p. 21)

Salvation does not come from an organization but only through a personal faith in the Lord Jesus Christ. In fact, if what the Watchtower teaches is true, it leaves many unsolved problems. If salvation is obtained through an "organization," one must determine which organization is the correct one.

However, there are *many* groups that claim to be the only channel through which God works. It is one thing to make such a claim but quite another to prove it. Interestingly, many of the various organizations which claim to be "the only way" seem to have so many teachings and practices in common.

In addition, if the present-day Watchtower society really is the true organization, then for years the society was not "the true organization" because it used to teach and practice many things which it now considers "pagan" and "false." Surely the true organization could not ignorantly have taught pagan and false teachings! If the original Watchtower organization, or the organization it became at any time along the way, was the true organization, then the *present* organization is not God's channel of truth because it differs so greatly from any of those of the past.

The Watchtower Society doesn't seem to have any "absolute truth," because what it considers to be truth keeps changing. Even today, what Jehovah's Witnesses believe could (and probably will) be changed sometime in the near future. If this occurs, any Witnesses who do not change their beliefs to agree with the new teachings will be disfellowshipped and considered "apostate." The Watchtower's "truth" never stays the same for very long. But absolute truth, real truth, never changes. Thus, the Watchtower Society can in no way be God's means of communicating to this earth.

Another fact that Jehovah's Witnesses ignore is that the church Christ founded and His disciples carried on was a pure church. Volumes of writings are available from early church history. Why then does God continually give the governing body of the Watchtower Society "new light"? If the "new light" that the Watchtower Society receives is not something the original church was aware of, there must have been a lot of important information that God did not reveal in times past. Why would He wait almost 2000 years to communicate truth if this new light is as important as the Watchtower claims?

But as we have demonstrated, the "new light" of the Watchtower is neither "new" nor "true." For anyone who wants to know "the truth," all he needs to do is read the

Bible. The Holy Spirit is the author of the Bible, and He will lead those who desire to know God's will into the truth. That is why there is unity among Bible-believing Christians on the essentials of salvation.

Do not be deceived. Neither the Watchtower nor any other organization can dispense salvation. Jesus said in John 14:6, "I am the way, the truth, and the life: no man cometh unto the Father, but by me."

The Bottom Line

If salvation came through an organization, man would have a problem knowing which one to choose, because these self-promoting groups are basically all the same. In various ways, they maintain that Jesus died only for the sins that we inherited from Adam, while one's own personal sins can only be removed through "good works" and endurance. But it is not just "good works" that these religions are interested in.

Such organizations define "good works" as being 100% in submission to their authority and following the rules and regulations that they proclaim. Of course, they never tell you that the rules might change tomorrow, so you will have to forget what you once learned and conform to the "new light" that will eventually come.

The Watchtower Society teaches that God operates only through its organization, and if you do not keep under its umbrella, God's most severe judgment will come upon you at Armageddon. For Jehovah's Witnesses this means that all who reject their message will be eternally annihilated at death and never given a second chance in the future world. As with most other religious groups, the future world becomes the reward for the faithful.

Never does a cult let you have any assurance as to your eternal condition. It teaches that you must endure to the end, and even after that you will be judged by God. Its adherents are constantly kept in fear. While it says it believes in a God of love, it teaches that God is vindictive to any who do not adhere to the "party line" right to the end. After people join these types of organizations and are less than satisfied, they are commonly told that they must try a little harder if they want to be satisfied. Everything is always based on "tomorrow."

Is this the way God intended it? No! God has never sought out only one organization to dispense His salvation. In fact, salvation does not come through an organization at all. Eternal salvation is found in Jesus Christ alone. Jesus said in John 14:6, "I am the way, the truth, and the life: no man cometh unto the Father but by me."

The way to the Father is very exclusive—only through the Lord Jesus Christ—but *all* are invited to come. In Matthew 11:28–30 Jesus said, "Come unto me, all ye that labour and are heavy laden, and I will give you rest. Take my yoke upon you, and learn of me; for I am meek and lowly in heart: and ye shall find rest unto your souls. For my yoke is easy, and my burden is light."

The biggest hurdle to salvation is not with God, but with ourselves. Christ can only save sinners. Yet most people do not consider themselves sinners; that label is only reserved for thieves, murderers, etc. But for most of us, it is not the gross outward sins we are guilty of, but the inward sins, like pride, ingratitude, selfishness, boasting, hypocrisy, covetousness, malice, jealousy, envy, strife, deceit, backbiting, gossip, hatefulness, lies, lust, evil thoughts, etc. It is not enough to say, "No one is perfect," or "We all make mistakes." We need to realize just how sinful we are and be willing to confess our sins.

If we admit our sins and are willing to confess them to God, asking the Lord Jesus Christ to come into our life to be our personal Savior, we will be forgiven. First John 1:9 says, "If we confess our sins, he is faithful and just to forgive us our sins, and to cleanse us from all unrighteousness." At that moment we will be born into the eternal family of God, become one of His blood-washed children, and our name will be written down in the "Lamb's Book of Life," which is our sure ticket to heaven.

Salvation is a free gift from God, not something to be achieved. Jesus said in John 10:28, "And I give unto them eternal life; and they shall never perish, neither shall any man pluck them out of my hand." Christ not only gives the gift of eternal life; He also keeps the believer through His mighty power for all eternity.

One very important truth we must remember is that when we come to Jesus Christ for salvation, we become His children and are born into the family of God. Yes, at times we may be disobedient children, but God does not cast us aside. Our fellowship with Him can be disrupted until we are willing to confess our sins and ask His forgiveness, but we are not cast off. We belong eternally to God.

Numerous religious groups object to this truth. "If you say that you are once and for all saved," they reply, "you must think you can go out and do whatever you want and still get to heaven! You can commit murder or adultery and still get to heaven!"

The fallacy of this argument is in not realizing that when

a person comes to Christ, he is *changed.* Before I came to Christ, I loved to sin. But when I realized that my sins sent Jesus Christ to die on the tree for me, I turned away from sinful behavior. Now I want to do what *pleases* God. I read the Bible, go to a gospel-preaching church to hear the Word, and pray so that I can know how God wants me to live. There will be times when I sin and displease my heavenly Father, but it is not something that I want to do, and I am greatly *distressed* when I do sin. If it were up to me, I would never sin again! So you see, if a person is really saved, he makes an about-face and no longer desires to sin but to walk in the way of holiness.

Others may object and say, "Yes, God is able to keep you, but what if you choose to walk away from Christ?" This kind of reasoning is impossible to understand. Until the age of fourteen I was a slave to Satan. I carried a heavy burden of sin. I was not satisfied. I had no real direction and purpose to my life. But when I finally realized what an ungodly, wicked sinner I was before God, I confessed my sins and asked the Lord Jesus Christ to be my Savior. When I did, this heavy burden of sin was removed. I was free from being a slave to Satan. I had direction and purpose in life. I now know what it means to be free! To think that I would ever want to go back and be a slave to Satan and take up that heavy burden of sin once again after I have known the marvelous thrill of experiencing the love of God is utterly incomprehensible.

Often I hear, "But there are so many churches, how do I know which one is right for me?" Yes, there are a lot of churches, but all Bible-believing, gospel-preaching churches uphold the basic fundamentals of Christianity. There is a variety to choose from. Some people like large churches, others like small ones. Some groups are rather formal and others less so. Choose the gospel-preaching church that you feel most comfortable in.

If you are not saved and do not have the assurance of eternal life in heaven when you die, I pray you will come to Jesus Christ, receive Him as your personal Savior, and become one of God's born-again children. When you do, you will live in constantly growing fellowship with Him on this earth and then spend all eternity with God in a perfect heaven.

Chapter Twelve

Growing Up as a Jehovah's Witness

*W*hat is it really like to grow up under the shadow of the Watchtower? The following testimony is a composite of five true stories of real people who were raised as Jehovah's Witnesses. Their experiences have been compiled as the story of just one person, whom we'll call Marlene.

It is hard for the average person to comprehend what growing up as a Jehovah's Witness is like. It is similar to growing up in a prison—but in a prison where the guards attempt to make you think you are really the freest person in the world. How is this possible? It is something that happens quite subtly. Many adults actually choose to enter this prison on their own free will! They simply don't take time to think, or they refuse to investigate and uncover the facts.

As a child, however, I had no choice in the matter; my parents made it for me. It was not until many years later that

I realized what had happened to me—to my mind, to my independence and to my inner strength. The realization was so painful to me that I wished I could die. But now I am getting ahead of the story.

I was born and raised in Pennsylvania. My life was quite normal until I was ten years old. My father had been out of work for a while, which caused a great deal of tension in my home. It was a "down time" in the life of my parents. One Saturday morning there was a knock at our door. My mother—with me hiding behind her—went to the door and found there two well-dressed, middle-aged people, a man and a woman, each carrying a briefcase.

They had broad smiles and seemed to be quite friendly. They explained that they were religious people who were interested in the welfare of others in the area. They declared that we were living in a very wicked world which would only become worse. Soon this *old* world system would pass away, and "just around the corner" this sin-cursed earth would become a beautiful paradise with no more crime, sickness or death. Everyone would live in beautiful homes with an abundance of delicious food at their beck and call.

Something in their voices made my mother listen intently. They also explained that only those people who were receptive to the Watchtower Society's message could stay alive to enter this new earth. They even had some beautiful pictures to show us, to give us an idea of what this paradise would look like. But anyone who did not listen to their message, they stated clearly, would die.

My mother was impressed with their friendliness. She called my father to join us, to hear what these people had to say. They explained that God worked only through an organization, and He had appointed the Watchtower Society to be "the sole channel of communication to this earth." If people wanted to have any contact with God and learn what He had to say, they had to become members of "God's organization." All those who would *not* listen would die at Armageddon and be eternally annihilated.

This all seemed very strange to me. I had been taught that God was a loving God, but now I was being told that at "the battle of Armageddon" God was going to destroy everyone who did not become a Jehovah's Witness.

The couple said they couldn't stay too long but would be back in the near future, if my parents were interested.

The next time they came, my father invited them in. They admired our house and told my parents what lovely children they had. (I had a brother who was four years younger than me.) I was a little shy over all this attention, but, of course, I enjoyed it. Together with my father and mother, I sat and listened to what these two seemingly sincere Witnesses had to say. I looked at their magazines. They pointed to the pictures that showed how Jehovah God would kill everyone who was not a member of His organization.

In the beginning my father asked most of the questions. I didn't always understand the answers that were given. My mother remarked that we already had a lovely life, and just as soon as her husband found a new job things would be even better. But one of the Jehovah's Witnesses asserted that it wouldn't last very long if we didn't join the Watchtower Society.

This was the beginning of months of a so-called "Bible study." Each week the two Witnesses came back and read their books to us. First they had my father or mother read a paragraph, then they would ask them a question pertaining to something they had just read. At the time, none of us realized that this was a subtle propagandizing method, but when we did, it was much too late.

My family became more and more involved in these "Watchtower book studies." The Jehovah's Witnesses kept pointing out the need to take a stand for Jehovah if we wished to survive the awful destruction at Armageddon. I was afraid! I had always been fearful about war, but the war they referred to would encompass the whole earth—no one was safe. So I listened to them. I wanted my family to quickly join the Jehovah's Witnesses so that none of us would die, including my younger brother.

My father eventually found a job. I thought that our family life would soon return to normal, but this never happened. Things were never the same after we allowed the two Witnesses to come into our home.

At the urging of this couple, we began attending meetings at the Kingdom Hall. At first we went to the two meetings on Sunday morning. During the first fifty minutes someone gave a "public talk," followed by a fifty-minute study of the *Watchtower* magazine. Later on, we started to attend the one-hour "book study" on Tuesday nights, and the "Theocratic Ministry School" and "Service Meeting" (each fifty minutes long) on Thursday nights.

I did not find this much fun, to say the least. Not only were the meetings extremely boring, but my father had to wear a suit and tie, and my mother her best dress—which had to come down over her knees. All us children had to dress exactly like the adults, and we were supposed to sit perfectly still all through these dry, lengthy meetings and act like adults at all times. Ugh, this was grueling! But as I look back on it, it was one of the easier parts of being a Jehovah's Witness.

After my father and mother were baptized at a big district convention in front of thousands of people, things began to get worse. My parents were now supposed to spend ten hours every month going door to door, and my brother and I had to accompany them. Once again, we had to put on our Sunday clothes and were always reminded to be on our best behavior. After all, we were now "ministers of Jehovah"—we were His representatives on earth and we had to give a "good impression."

We were taught how to give a Watchtower Society "sales pitch" and especially how to urge people to buy the *Awake!* and *Watchtower* magazines. (At this time they were sold. Later the society simply asked for a donation in order to escape paying sales tax.) I always hated going from door to door, because we met a lot of indignant people and had a lot of doors slammed in our faces. At times we went to the homes of some of the children I knew from school. This was always embarrassing.

Slowly my parents began to forbid me from being involved in everyday activities. For example, I could no longer go to my friends' birthday parties. And one week before my eleventh birthday, my mother announced—as if it was an accepted thing—that *my* birthday would no longer be celebrated either! I cried, and felt that I was no longer worth anything! We had always had lovely birthday celebrations with beautifully decorated cakes and a number of presents. I asked my mother why we could not celebrate my birthday, and she explained that in Bible times when someone once celebrated his birthday, a good man got beheaded. She also declared that there was nothing in the Bible about Jesus and his apostles celebrating their birthdays.

We children were also forbidden to celebrate Christmas—and all other holidays. They were considered pagan by the Watchtower Society, and "true Christians" should not have anything to do with heathen practices. But this explanation did not ease the sorrow in my heart.

Having Christmas taken away was bad, but going back to school after the holidays was much worse. The teacher always asked what presents we had received. I pressed my cold, sweaty hands together, waiting for my turn to answer. When I said "nothing," it felt like my heart would break. I almost fainted. I could feel everyone looking at me. I felt different, and then their gossip began. Some whispered: "It's because she is a Jehovah's Witness." I had to go home—I could not take any more! So I said, "I have a pain in my stomach" and I was allowed to leave.

Another humiliating decree of the Watchtower Society was that we could not salute the flag. Each morning, as the other students stood up to salute the flag, I would remain seated in my chair. Everyone looked at me. I wished there was some way I could disappear, but there was no place to hide. And these stares did not just occur in the classroom. Word got around about this "strange" girl, and others would look at me in the hallways and on the playground. I never felt included in anything at school; I felt isolated and different.

This hit me even harder when I learned that sometimes when the adult Witnesses attended public functions, they would stand for the saluting of the flag or the national anthem so as not look conspicuous. But as children, we had no option—we remained seated in school!

From that Christmas on, school was never the same again. Everyone looked at me as if I were odd, and that's how I saw myself. Different, different, different. A grownup might be able to bear it, but not a child. (My brother too, four grades behind me, was sometimes taunted.) There were only two children in my class who would come near me.

No matter what the activity was outside the classroom, when I asked my mother if I could participate, I was always told it wasn't good, because it could lead to one thing or another. It seemed as if *everything* except going to the Kingdom Hall was dangerous!

My mother persuaded me to stop sports, because it involved too much time. She claimed there were better things to do. For example, we could sit together and read the *Watchtower* magazine and underline the answers to the questions that would be asked at the "Watchtower Study" on Sunday morning. The more questions we answered, the more "spiritual" we were.

The answers were always given in the magazine. We could never come up with our own answers or even ask unauthorized questions. They were taboo. I never could understand why no one ever voiced any really thought-provoking questions or gave an answer different than what was found in the book. When I asked once, I was told that this is the way Jehovah wanted it. Of course, no Bible verse was offered to prove this.

When someone from my school had a party, I could never go because of "what could happen," even though the grownups would never explain what that meant. A girl who had been a close friend of mine since I started school stopped asking me to go with her to the parties. She knew what the answer would be; and she also didn't share with me how much fun the parties had been. She knew me well enough to know how painful it was not to be a part of a group. Despite the fact that she was only thirteen, she knew I was caught in a trap. (I guess I knew it too, because I remember how she looked at me from time to time.) She never said anything unkind, but often reminded me how she would like us to continue to be friends.

But my parents formulated various reasons why I could seldom be with her. She was one of those from the "outside"—which means anyone who is not a Jehovah's Witness. They considered her to be from the devil and said she would soon die, when Armageddon occurred, which was always just around the corner. All such people were purported to mislead others, desiring to make people "as evil as themselves." They had no scruples, my father asserted.

One day I was quite upset because I couldn't spend the night at my friend's home, something I had often done before our family became Witnesses. But I was again told that I might become involved—without being aware of it—in something that Jehovah didn't like. Young people especially could "get up to so much."

Curious, I asked what it was we could "get up to," because the only things we girls ever did was watch television, read magazines, or sit and talk.

"Even their magazines can be a bad influence," my mother said, and television too, with its morally corrupt programs. The things we might gab about and the people who maybe would drop in at my friend's house—what type were they?

My mother had never acted like this *before,* because my parents knew Jane's parents very well and had always maintained they were "good people."

When Jane turned thirteen, I sent her a secret birthday present. After that I lay under my blanket and asked Jehovah to forgive me for what I had done. I hoped to receive some kind of a sign that Jehovah had forgiven me, so that I could still look forward to everlasting life which might come at the end of the Millennium. But I never received any sign.

I never felt the connection to Jehovah that Witnesses told me I would feel when I prayed. Never! I was afraid that He did not like me, and that one day I would lose my life with the blinded people from the "outside." For a while I prayed several times a day in the hope that I might reach Jehovah.

At this time I had a very frightening experience that I will never forget. My mother needed an operation, and I knew a Jehovah's Witness is not allowed to receive a blood transfusion, even if a lot of blood is lost.

I had heard that should a Jehovah's Witness choose to have a transfusion, the elders would post people at the hospital to make sure the patient did not receive any blood. It was not a matter of choice or conscience, but a command from the society.

I knew this could lead to my mother's death. I did not want her to die—in spite of all the difficulties I was now facing growing up in a Jehovah's Witness home. I was so relieved when my mother returned safely home after the operation.

As I grew older, it was expected that I would become more adept at preaching door to door. I now had to present "the true message," as it was called. A "new world order" was supposed to arrive on earth—at the latest, by October 1975—but all non-Jehovah's Witnesses were supposed to die first. The time left to preach this message was very short. We heard this over and over again, at every meeting. We read it in our literature, and nobody doubted its truth. Everyone who became a Jehovah's Witness had the ability to achieve everlasting life at the end of the Millennium if he or she proved faithful and God felt they were "worthy."

Many of the Witnesses I knew then sold everything they owned a year or two prior to 1975, because now Judgment Day was close at hand! Several people sold their homes and moved into cheap apartments so they could give up their jobs and use all their time to convert other people. Just before 1975, when everyone was looking forward to Judgment Day, most of the Witnesses were in a frenzy and tried to convert as many people as possible.

The Watchtower Society even went so far as to tell those of us who were in high school not to complete our education, because we would never finish it, with so few months left before 1975. If, instead, we became pioneers, using all our time to preach, our future would be safe.

As a young and rather shy Jehovah's Witness, I was almost always content just to show our magazines, to see if people would read one. If I was successful, my conscience was relieved. It was understood that Jehovah, although unseen, accompanied Jehovah's Witnesses whenever we visited other people. We supposedly received Jehovah's nod of acceptance when we shared Watchtower material. This would influence us to do even better.

If you didn't sell anything, it was quite disappointing. (By the way, we always called it "disposing," because Jehovah's

Witnesses never "sell" their literature. The word "sell" is ta-boo in that connection.) But at various times I became an eager "preacher" and got someone to listen and accept my explanation. I had practiced a lot.

I must admit, however, that I seldom used the Bible as a reference, because it seemed to me that many of the biblical texts that were recommended didn't apply clearly to the Watchtower material. Besides, our literature *was* our refer-ence, so it might as well be sufficient for outsiders. If a state-ment was included in the organization's books and maga-zines, it was *law*—and a Witness should never question it. That would be the same as interrogating Jehovah God Him-self!

If it happened that a member of the congregation began to express doubts, other members became very watchful of this person. It was a sign that Satan was getting a grip on the doubter and poisoning his or her mind. That poison could no doubt spread to other Witnesses and make them doubt-ful as well. So even those things that seemed wrong to me about my faith, I kept to myself. I didn't want anyone to think less of me. I wanted to be considered an "insider," so that I could be sure of surviving Judgment Day when Jeho-vah came with His big sword.

At other times I couldn't force myself out of the house to go and witness to people. Too often they told me, "We're doing fine." I could see that, but it was my job to make them understand that they weren't doing fine in the *right way*! You are not considered a true Jehovah's Witness if you don't go out and preach from door to door—because you then have no numbers to write on your monthly activity form, indicating that you had spoken with a set number of people. How many hours had you preached? How many books and magazines had you disposed of? This monthly form enabled the "elders" (those men who are the most spiritually "mature"), to determine, presumably, how mature the rest of us were. If you had spent less than ten hours a month visiting people and preaching to them, you weren't considered "mature."

If this slackness persisted over a period of time, the elders would step in and attempt to correct the spiritual climate of that wayward Witness. The expression "You have to make that goal" followed me all my days as a Jehovah's Witness, and maybe it will for the rest of my life.

Regardless of a person's excuse, such as trying to live one's life without constant door-to-door solicitation—or if you did not agree with the elder's outlook—you were given a lecture about the importance of reaching your potential. All Witnesses had to strive toward this same goal of ten hours of preaching a month, regardless of their individual circumstances.

In the end I finally believed that whatever our leaders said was true. With the literature they had in hand, these elders were able to distort and change everything that was natural for a person to think and feel—so whatever the elders prescribed seemed to be the correct thing to do.

So much time was spent praying, getting ready for meetings, being at the meetings and going out "preaching," that there was little time for anything else, and I became a somber adult at the age of fourteen.

My younger brother was no longer as wild and full of tricks as he had once been. Our parents had made a big effort to subdue him, scolding him all the time. It was especially critical that he be quiet in the Kingdom Hall. Children had to sit quietly for two hours. It was very difficult, especially for my brother, who was small and often quite fidgety in the evenings. But there was no getting around it. To create a disturbance at a meeting was a sign that one didn't appreciate the word of Jehovah. When my brother did cause a disturbance, he'd be taken outside by my father and chastised.

We had to wear our best clothes when we attended the meetings at the Kingdom Hall. My brother could not wear jeans, which he otherwise wore. Now he had to wear "nice clothes." As a result, children looked identical to grownups, whose clothes looked like full-dress uniforms. Always a suit, elegant trousers, and jacket and tie. Never sweat suits and tennis shoes. No! "*Nice* shoes"—the type you can polish and make shiny. I was absolutely forbidden to attend meetings wearing slacks, despite my protests that I had never worn a dress and didn't feel comfortable in one.

I might as well have been talking to the wall. No one was interested in what I thought. I always wore dresses when we attended meetings—of a certain length, of course. Trousers were for men. Short dresses only awakened men's appetites. Women and girls were not to show themselves off. Since they were considered inferior to men, women were expected to adapt to men.

My mother changed drastically. She became a very quiet person, always devotedly asking my father before she ever proceeded with anything. Father made all the decisions. At both the Kingdom Hall and in the volumes of Watchtower literature, we were told that men were "masters" over women, and it was the husband who made the decisions in the home.

A woman could discuss an issue, but the man always had the last word. If a woman did not obey her husband in everything, it was considered worse than being a worldly nonbeliever.

The Watchtower literature often reminded us that God first created Adam. Eve, fashioned from one of Adam's ribs, came second. This proved that women were inferior to men and should be subordinate to them. No woman could ever speak publicly at a meeting, and no one ever tried.

This was the way my mother now lived. She realized that this was the only way. She was taught to believe that, as a woman, when she was given an order, she was to obey.

Previously I had seen my mother as a free and happy person who willingly participated in a number of activities. She was the one we always went to when we needed something. She would fix everything in her energetic way. Now she asked my father before proceeding with anything, and the dictum of the Watchtower Society was always considered whenever they were unsure of what to do.

It didn't feel like we were living anymore. We had become slaves, robots, blindly accepting orders from higher-ups—from the organization. The orders were law and had to be obeyed. The rules and regulations were reinforced over and over in Watchtower literature. The society told us these were "Jehovah's laws" that were passed on by His chosen organization, which was indwelt by His special Spirit in order to declare His will to all members. It was understood that our leaders had a direct line to God. Disobedience against the organization was the same thing as sinning against Jehovah. One had to follow the "party line" or be punished.

Many times we saw members of our community excluded. If a Witness refused to do as commanded by the society, even in the smallest matter—like daring to send a birthday card to someone, or a Christmas card—and refused to repent when reprimanded, he or she was thrown out. I remember very clearly a young man who was given a public warning. It was announced from the speaker's chair that this person had done something improper and that now he had to make amends. This warning apparently did not have the effect the leaders wished, and one evening at a later meeting they said that he was "disfellowshipped."

I knew what that meant, and I sat stiffly in my chair with sweaty hands as I heard this proclamation read. The hall became very quiet. I looked cautiously around, but there was no sign of him. Suddenly I noticed his mother sitting by herself, crying quietly. I would have loved to have been able to console her, but I did not know how to do this. Her son was condemned to social death in the Watchtower Society. Is there any consolation adequate for that?

Each person now knew what to do. His was not just banishment from the Kingdom Hall, but from everyone who had a connection to the Watchtower Society. None of us was permitted to have anything to do with him, not even his parents. If we did, we would become a party to his great sin—whatever it was.

This young man, whom I didn't know very well (but enough to see that he was a quiet person who couldn't hurt a fly), was now all alone. As a Jehovah's Witness he had no real friends outside the organization because he, like all of us, had always been strongly discouraged from associating with "Satan's children."

A week or so after his expulsion I met him by chance on

the street one day. It happened suddenly, and I wasn't prepared when he turned up in the crowd. We had almost walked past each other when I first saw him. For only a moment I met his eyes, and I could see him yearning for understanding and human contact. But I was with another Jehovah's Witness friend. Duty bound, I quickly turned my face away, something a good Jehovah's Witness should do when he or she meets someone who has had been expelled. I knew that this "disfellowshipped" person was as good as dead.

Jehovah's Witnesses are taught that Jehovah kills "outsiders" with His sword on the day of reckoning at Armageddon. Suddenly, this young man found himself awaiting judgment, and the Watchtower organization was the power behind it. We shunned him completely.

Later, I learned that he left home about a month after his expulsion. No one talked about him openly, though there was a lot of whispered gossip at the Kingdom Hall. Some said his family was continuing to help him because he was still in school, though he began skipping class. Otherwise, there was no contact with him. It was his own fault. His parents had to protect their own cleanliness and innocence by refraining from seeing him.

By listening to the gossip, I found out that he had started smoking and that this resulted in his expulsion. About six months later word got out he had begun to drink, and much later that he had become a drug addict. One time he came home in a terrible state, but his parents would help him only if he promised to commit himself to the organization again. When he said he couldn't do that, they shunned him completely. Someone said that he died a short time later, probably from an overdose.

I later discovered that this process of shunning an individual causes many Jehovah's Witnesses to go deep into sin. The Watchtower Society's philosophy is that you are either a "clean" Jehovah's Witness or a "dirty" sinner. There is no middle ground. You can't be a morally clean person and not be a Jehovah's Witness. For this reason, when someone leaves or is disfellowshipped, he or she often feels so lost that they fall headlong into the sins of the world.

It was at this point, for the first time, that I could see that something was radically wrong with the Watchtower Society. I didn't know this young man well, but I grieved over him in a strange way. There was an anger in my sorrow that I hadn't previously known.

The great love that Jehovah's Witnesses boast about was clearly not evident in this situation. They may love the "faithful," but this is always conditional, because they are quite willing to betray one another over the slightest matter. They feel it is their duty to the organization to inform on one another.

If someone is discovered doing something that the organization could not accept, other members feel guilty if they don't inform the elders—even if it involves their closest friend, or their child, father, mother, grandparents or grandchildren. There's no way to get around it. Those most in need of support and acceptance are ostracized; and the only way back is when they are willing to repent of their deeds and allow themselves to be molded back into the rules and regulations of the Watchtower Society.

These were terrible thoughts for me to think. It felt like a landslide . . . all these thoughts . . . and I tried to suppress them time after time, as I had been taught to do. We had been told that these types of thoughts are evil and from the devil. I couldn't even talk to my parents about my terrible thoughts. I knew what their response would be: They would read to me out of our magazines the standard answers that existed for every question. It was simple. No one had to think for himself. In this way the faith remained the same for all Jehovah's Witnesses. It was important that we all agreed, and if someone didn't, they were forced to be disfellowshipped.

I tried to concentrate more on the Watchtower literature. I even tried to convert some of my school friends. My best friend listened to me, on and off, when I talked about my religion, but I had the impression she did it only because she felt sorry for me.

I made up my mind not to reveal my feelings about my religion to her. These kinds of conversations took too much out of me, and I could no longer afford it. We weren't that close anymore, because there was so little we could do together. (My parents were convinced that my friend watched sinful films on TV and at the cinema, and all parties, according to my mother, were orgies of drinking and sex.) Almost everything was branded sinful by the Watchtower Society.

But this bothered me. I knew that some young Jehovah's Witnesses hosted parties with dancing and drinking. I even heard that some of the teens became drunk, but the parents covered it up because the party was held at the home of a Jehovah's Witness. So, how could parties at other people's houses be any worse than those I had heard about among the Jehovah's Witnesses?

When I discussed this with my mother and suggested that I should ask some of my school friends what their parties were like, my parents said it wasn't worth asking. "Outsiders" can't be trusted; they would try to lead me astray. A true Witness must expect that from the world.

About this time a very strange thing happened. The congregation wanted to honor one of the elders, but birthdays were forbidden because they were considered pagan. However, the Witnesses found a way to work around this. They called it an "anniversary" party. It didn't seem to bother anyone, at least outwardly, that the event fell on the exact day of this elder's birthday. They had an "anniversary" cake with candles and presents, and of course there was the usual dancing and drinking that goes along with Jehovah's Witnesses' parties. Even as a young person I could see through the hypocrisy, but it didn't seem to bother the others—it gave them an opportunity to have a party!

I felt that we would always be Jehovah's Witnesses. After all, my parents seemed so enamored with everything the Watchtower Society said. They claimed that it was the only organization that had "the truth," and everyone else was from the devil. But then something happened that completely changed my circumstances and led me to the true meaning of life.

Chapter Thirteen

Finding the True Meaning of Life

Both my mother's father and brother died quite unexpectedly in the same year, which proved to be terribly traumatic for my mother. Shortly afterward, her younger brother committed suicide (a hideous sin to a Jehovah's Witness). My mother was completely humiliated. She also began to have doubts about what happens after death. Since the Watchtower Society promises its followers that Armageddon is just around the corner, most of them believe they will never die but will go directly onto the new earth. Therefore, the Watchtower Society doesn't do much to prepare people for death.

This caused my mother a lot of emotional pain. Not only was she wrestling with the problem of what happens after death, but she was left to grieve alone. The other Witnesses just seemed to shy away from her. She sensed there was something wrong with the Watchtower Society, even though she couldn't put her finger on it.

Before long she stopped attending the Kingdom Hall. For about a year afterward my father faithfully took us to the meetings. But gradually it became too much for him, and we stopped going altogether. The elders visited from time to time to convince my mother and father to attend. They refused. As a result, Mom and Dad were disfellowshipped.

My grandmother and aunt, however, continued to be faithful Witnesses, so when my father and mother were shunned, they followed the "party line" and completely disassociated from us. This blow was hard on us all, but particularly on my mother. For about two years we had no religious affiliation at all.

When I was nineteen, I met a young man, and we started dating. He was from a Christian background, so I visited the church where he and his parents attended. Even though I had not gone to the Kingdom Hall for over two years, it was hard at first. Jehovah's Witnesses are taught that if we enter a Christian church, Satan is waiting at the entrance and will pounce on us, forcing us to become demon-possessed. Naturally, this did not occur, but I was initially quite afraid.

I was also wary of the large cross at the front of the church. Jehovah's Witnesses are taught that the cross is a "pagan" symbol and that Christians worship the cross. It took me a while to become accustomed to it. Eventually I learned the truth: Born-again Christians do not worship the cross. Rather, it is a reminder that the Lord Jesus Christ died in order to take away our sins, just as Communion reminds people of Christ's death. The cross is a reminder of God's great love, for He sacrificed His Son for all people and saves all who receive Jesus as their Savior.

The services at the Christian church were much different from the meetings at the Kingdom Hall. The singing was lively and heartfelt; people seemed to know why they were singing. Conversely, the songs of the Kingdom Hall were slow and without feeling. At the Christian church the pastor taught from the Bible in every message, often studying each verse of a certain book of the Bible over a period of time. He never simply read to the congregation from standard printed material. At this Christian church Jesus seemed to be the central focus of all the messages and songs, while at the Kingdom Hall the main emphasis was on Jehovah.

I realize now how immensely influenced I had been by the teachings at the Kingdom Hall. The Christian perspective is just about the opposite of the Jehovah's Witnesses. In addition, Watchtower publications often do not tell the truth about the beliefs of born-again, Bible-believing Christians.

For example, the concept of personal sin was totally foreign to me. Jehovah's Witnesses are taught that we are not as awful sinners as those on the "outside," though we know we are not perfect. The Bible-believing churches, however, emphasize that we are *all* ungodly, wicked sinners and that we deserve eternal punishment. We are born in sin and have a sin nature, and are responsible to God for our actions. At the Kingdom Hall we used to compare ourselves to people we felt were worse sinners, but the Bible compares us to a holy and righteous God and thus clearly shows us how sinful we are before Him. At first I found it difficult to face up to my own personal sins and sin nature.

But probably the hardest concept to grapple with was the doctrine of the Trinity, which The Watchtower Society completely denies. In their minds the worst sin a person can commit is to believe that God, though only one, exists in three equal and distinct persons. But as I slowly came to understand from the Bible the meaning of the Trinity, I realized that the Watchtower Society had greatly perverted the truth. I still do not understand why it took this stance and brainwashed its followers against it.

Time passed. I was married, and started a family. Even though I had been attending church for almost four years, had accepted the doctrines and teachings of traditional Christianity, and told people I was a Christian, I still felt something was missing. I did not feel a true sense of peace and joy that I thought should accompany true Christianity.

At this time my husband and I began to attend a new church. At that very first service I realized I needed to make a personal commitment to Jesus Christ. It wasn't simply a matter of accepting the teachings of Christ with my head and being moral in my actions; I also desperately needed a personal relationship with Him. I realized just how sinful my heart was before God. I also understood that Jesus had died for me personally. I saw that it was through the shed blood of the Lord Jesus Christ that my sins could be forgiven and I could come into a personal relationship with God.

As I confessed my many sins and asked Jesus to be my personal Savior, the burden of sin I had been carrying for so long was taken away. In its place I was given eternal life and personally experienced the love, joy and peace that only God can give. As I relinquished my own sense of goodness as a means of salvation and put my faith and trust in Jesus Christ as my own personal Savior, I found what I had been longing for all my life.

When I asked Jesus Christ to be my Savior, the Holy Spirit, who truly is a Person, came into my life to dwell with me. As I began to read the Bible, it became a living book through the guidance of the Holy Spirit. As I have continued attending church, reading my Bible daily and, by the grace of God, putting into practice the things I have learned from the Word of God, I have grown in the things of the Lord.

I don't know why it took me so many years to find Jesus Christ, but I am thankful I can now live in fellowship with the Triune God while on this earth. At the very moment I die, I will go immediately to heaven and be there for all eternity.

Let me summarize my growing up a Jehovah's Witness in this way: At the time my parents became Jehovah's Witnesses, something was taken away from me, which was my life. From that time and until Jesus found me, my life felt vague and disconnected. I felt *alienated* and *abnormal*.

Life was like walking down a long, dark hallway. There was no one else there. I felt all alone. There was just a feeling of hopelessness, and a deep hurt inside my heart and soul that nothing could penetrate or heal. Since I was out of touch with who I was, life could not bring me any real joy or happiness.

For the typical Jehovah's Witness, happiness, along with plenty of other normal feelings, is put on hold until the "New Order" (the new earth) comes into existence. We were taught that every negative thought, feeling or action is the devil's doing. We were told to put our trust in Jehovah. Life was like being on a pony ride, going round and round in a circle and getting nowhere. There was only fear and sadness, and wishing for Armageddon when I was in the Watchtower Society. How bleak! How cold!

How does it feel to remain seated during the flag saluting? It is like being on stage: all eyes are upon you, wondering what your next move will be.

Embarrassed? Yes.

Humiliated? Of course.

Understood? Never.

How can anyone understand when you are able to provide no answers to their questions? All we could give them was an obscure line from a Watchtower publication. There's no way to relate to others because they can't relate to you. Withdrawing into one's self happens regularly because there is nowhere else to go.

The world of the Watchtower is divided into "good" versus "bad," and one had better be on the right side at Armageddon, which is "just around the corner." I could trust no one, feared everyone, and could love only the chosen few. I had been reaching out for years but never came close. I could not connect with others because I was continually judging them. It kept me fearful, angry and judgmental.

We were taught that we are the "chosen ones," because we would live on after everyone else was destroyed by the horrifying destruction known as Armageddon. For this reason, we could not mingle with the wrong people or become attached to "worldly ones"—don't feel for them, only condemn them to eternal destruction. Can you understand how powerful the words "total destruction" make a child feel?

Those with emotional distress are not shown acceptance or compassion, only judgment. All hope, all faith, all everlasting life lay within God's organization, the Watchtower

Society, not through Jesus. This thought was implanted in my mind so that nothing else could enter.

Being a member of the Jehovah's Witnesses always made me feel unworthy. I felt like God's finger was always pointed at me. I was not allowed any normal feelings or emotions; many times I thought I would be better off dead. Then, perhaps, I'd find forgiveness, another life, or at least reclaim the one I had lost. I wondered if there was anything that could possibly fill the void in my heart.

Life unfolded around me, but I did not feel a part of it. I went through the motions of living, but felt dead inside. I was constantly looking over my shoulder to see if anyone was watching, sometimes feeling like someone was stalking me, just waiting for me to make a wrong move. (This was not just a feeling, but was actually true.) I soon realized that I was *no one*, just a part of one big mass of people who seem to believe as I did. I wasn't an individual but an extension of an organization that denied my suffering. And if I really was suffering, it was for "God's organization" and therefore warranted.

It's true I felt connected to other Jehovah's Witnesses, but only because I felt so rejected by everyone else. The only direction in which I could move was the one given me by the Watchtower Society. They told me what I should or shouldn't do, but omitted the *how* or *why*. It is a dictatorship; I needed permission to do just about everything. "Have faith," they told me, but they didn't give me any truth to believe in. Only false hope, broken promises and shattered dreams.

I didn't feel right inside, and when I asked for an explanation, I only received a slap in the face. I had no mind of my own and could not make any decisions for myself.

As far as forgiveness was concerned, only a small group of men are given the power to forgive others. They decide who is truly remorseful—by putting you on stage for all to see. "God's organization" interprets the Bible and its meaning. There is no truth but theirs. No questions can be asked. They are "God's light" and "truth"—the *only* way to salvation. Meeting attendance and door-to-door preaching keeps members "in touch" with God's organization. They believe *only* the leaders. The rest are liars.

Is there really something better, or is this all there is?

I didn't think this was all there was, but I didn't know where to turn. I didn't know Jesus. He had been kept from me, hidden away in an obscure corner.

What was this organization that had such authority over me, so much control? They told me it was the truth. If so, why did I feel as if I were inside a deep well searching for truth?

One day, however, *Light* did find me in that deep, dark well. Light reached in, and I was ready to crawl out. The Light was also there to catch me if I should start to fall back in. That Light was *Jesus.*

I felt a great sense of comfort. No more walking alone. It took so long to come to this realization, and I will never again let any person or organization lead me away from the real truth as found in Jesus Christ.

It is said that *truth begins with a broken heart.* There is no doubt that mine was broken.

I thank Jesus that He showed me the light, the truth and the way. Jesus has mended my broken heart. He has shown me who I am. I am one of His children. He is my only Redeemer.

After all these years I now realize there is no going back; thanks to Jesus, I can move forward. I *know* that Jesus will always be there for me.

Appendix A

Why Was the Watchtower Society Associated with the UN?

Many were shocked and surprised when it was revealed in 2001 that the Watchtower Society had been a member of the nongovernmental organization (NGO) of the UN for ten years. The Watchtower Society has identified the United Nations with the idolatrous "image" of the scarlet-colored wild beast of Revelation.

The Watchtower book *Revelation—Its Grand Climax At Hand!* published in 1988, states on pages 248–9,

> The UN is actually a blasphemous counterfeit of God's Messianic Kingdom by his Prince of Peace, Jesus Christ—to whose princely rule there will be no end. (Isaiah 9:6, 7) Even if the UN were to patch up some temporary peace, wars would soon erupt again. This is in the nature of sinful men. "Their names have not been written upon the scroll of life from the founding of the world." Jehovah's Kingdom by Christ will not only establish eternal peace on earth but, on the basis of Jesus' ransom sacrifice, raise the dead, the righteous and the unrighteous who are in God's memory. (John 5:28, 29; Acts 24:15) This includes everyone who has remained

steadfast despite the attacks of Satan and his seed, and others who have yet to show themselves obedient. Obviously, God's scroll of life will never contain the names of die-hard adherents of Babylon the Great or of any who continued to worship the wild beast.—Exodus 32:33; Psalm 86:8-10; John 17:3; Revelation 16:2; 17:5.

The Watchtower book *Isaiah's Prophecy – Light For All Mankind*, Volume 1 (2000) states on pages 153–154,

> **Whom will Jehovah use** to discipline rebellious Christendom? We find the answer in the 17ᵗʰ chapter of Revelation. There we are introduced to a harlot, "Babylon the Great," representing all the world's false religions, including Christendom. The harlot is riding a scarlet-colored wild beast that has seven heads and ten horns. (Revelation 17:3, 5, 7–12) **The wild beast represents the united nations organization.** Will Jehovah's faithful Witnesses perish along with Babylon the Great? No. God is not displeased with them. Pure worship will survive. However, **the wild beast that destroys Babylon the Great also casts a greedy eye in the direction of Jehovah's people. In doing so, the beast carries out, not God's thought, but the thought of someone else. Who? Satan the Devil.**

While the Watchtower Society was condemning the UN, it was still a member of the NGO. Here is the list of requirements in order to belong to the NGO.

CRIITERIA FOR ASSOCIATION
WITH THE DEPARTMENT OF PUBLIC INFORMATION

The NGO must support and respect the principles of the Charter of the United Nations;

The NGO must be of recognized national or international standing;

The NGO should operate solely on a not-for-profit basis and have tax-exempt status;

The NGO must have the commitment of the means to conduct

effective information programs with its constituents and to a broader audience about UN activities by publishing newsletters, bulletins and pamphlets; organizing conferences, seminars and round table; or enlisting the attention of the media;

The NGO should have a satisfactory record of collaboration with UN Information centers/Services or other parts of the UN System prior to association;

The NGO should provide an audited annual financial statement, conducted by a qualified, independent accountant.

Note that the Watchtower Corporation must support and respect the principles of the Charter of the United Nations. This charter allows the UN to authorize the use of military force which the Watchtower Society was supposedly against.

Here is the first reaction of the Watchtower Society when it had been made public that it was a member of the NGO. (The *Guardian* was the publication where this information was first made available.)

JEHOVAH'S WITNESSES
OFFICE OF PUBLIC INFORMATION

October 22, 2001

Letters Editor
The Guardian

Dear Sir.
Stephen Bates' article in *The Guardian* of October 8 and 15 substantially misrepresents the background to Jehovah's Witnesses registration with the United Nations and contains a number of factual errors.

In 1991 one of our legal corporations registered with the United Nations as a NGO (non-governmental organization) for the sole purpose of getting access to the extensive library of the United Nations. This enabled a writer, who received an identification card, to enter their library for research purposes and to obtain information that has been used in writing articles in our journals about the United Nations. There was nothing secret about it.

At the time of the initial application no signature was required on the form. Years later, unbeknown to the Governing Body of Jehovah's Witnesses, the United Nations published "Criteria for Association", stipulating that affiliated NGO's are required to support the goals of the United Nations.

After learning of the situation, our membership as NGO was withdrawn and the ID card of the writer was returned.

Sincerely,

Paul Gillies
Press Officer for Jehovah's Witnesses in Britain.

In reality the society did not withdraw its membership until after this information was made public that it was a member of the NGO.

Here is a letter sent out by the Watchtower Society to all branch offices concerning this situation.

WORLD HEADQUARTERS OF JEHOVAH'S WITNESSES
25 Columbia Heights, Brooklyn, NY 11201-2483 Tel. 718-560-5000

November 1, 2001

Branch Committee

Dear Brothers:

Because of published allegations by opposers that we have secret links with the United Nations, a number of branches have inquired about the matter we have replied [*sic*]. This circular letter replaces any replies we have given earlier and is sent to all branches. To anyone inquiring within your branch territory you might respond according to what is stated below:

Our purpose for registering with the department of Public Information as a nongovernmental organization (NGO) in 1991 was to have access to research material available on health, ecological, and social problems at the United Nations library facilities. We had been using the library for many years prior to 1991, but in that year it became necessary to register as an NGO to have continued access. Registration papers filed with the United Nations that we have on file contain no statement that conflict [*sic*] with our Christian beliefs. Moreover, NGOs are informed by the United Nations that "association of NGOs with the DPI does not constitute their incorporation into the United Nations system, nor does it entitle associated organizations or their staff to any kind of privileges, immunities or special status."

Still, the Criteria for Association of NGOs—at least in their latest version—contain language that we cannot subscribe to. When we realized this, we immediately withdrew our registration. We are grateful that this matter was brought to our attention.

We trust that the above, is helpful in counteracting the attempts of opposers to discredit us.

Please be assured of our warm Christian love and best wishes.

Your brothers,

Chairman's Committee

c: Administration Offices Desks
Legal Department

Office of Public Information.

The Watchtower Society has a rather strange way of thinking! It was doing something that was inconsistent by claiming the UN was being used by Satan and still it was a part of that organization. Wasn't it saying one thing and doing something else? However, when this situation was pointed out to the society (the society was obviously in error because it changed its policy right away when this was pointed out), instead of being thankful that someone brought this to its attention, it did not thank them and consider them a friend of the society, but rather accused them of being "opposers."

So many letters were written to the NGO Section at the UN concerning the situation with the Watchtower Society that the Department of Public Information drew up a form letter to send to those who inquired:

DEPARTMENT OF PUBLIC INFORMATION

DPI   NGO

NON-GOVERNMENTAL ORGANIZATIONS

SECTION

United Nations, DPI/NGO Resource Centre, Room L-1B-31

Tel: (212)963-7223, 7234, 7078 ∑ FaxL212)963-2819 ∑ E-maii:dpingo@un.org

4 March 2004

To Whom It May Concern,

Recently the NGO Section has been receiving numerous inquires regarding the association of the **Watchtower Bible and Tract Society of New York** with the Department of Public Information (DPI*)*. This organization applied for association with DPI in 1991 and was granted association in 1992. By accepting association with the DPI, the organization agreed to meet criteria for association, including support and respect of the principles of the Charter of the United Nations and commitment and means to conduct effective information programmes with its constituents and to broader audience about the UN activities.

In October 2001, the Main Representative of the **Watchtower Bible and Tract Society of New York** to the United Nations, Giro Aulicino, requested termination of its association with DPI. Following this request, the DPI made a decision to disassociate the **Watchtower Bible and Tract Society of New York** as of 9 October 2001.

Please be informed that it is the policy of the Department of Public Information of the United Nations to keep correspondence between the United Nations and the NGOs associated with DPI confidential. However, please see below the paragraph included in all letters sent to NGOs approved for association in 1992.

"The principal purpose of association of Non-governmental organizations with the United Nations Department of Public Information is the redissemination of information in order to increase public understanding of the principles, activities and achievements of the United Nation and its Agencies. Consequently, it is important that you should keep us informed about your organization's information programme as it relates to the United Nations, including sending us issues of your relevant publications. We are enclosing a brochure of the 'The United Nations and Non-Governmental Organizations,' which will give you some information regarding the NGO relationship."

In addition, the criteria for NGOs to become associated with DPI include the following:

* that the NGO share the principles of the UN Charter;
* operate solely on a not-for-profit basis;
* have a demonstrated interest in United Nations issues and a proven ability to reach large or specialized audiences, such as educators, media representatives, policy makers and the business community;

- have the commitment and means to conduct effective information programmes about UN activities by publishing news letters, bulletins and pamphlets, organizing conferences, seminars and round tables; and enlisting the cooperation of the media.

We expect that you will share this information with your concerned colleagues, as we are unable to address the scores of duplicate requests regarding the Watchtower Bible and Tract Society that are being directed to our office. Thank you for your interest in the work of the United Nations.

Sincerely,

Paul Hoeffel
Chief NGO Section
Department of Public Information

Let us look at the two main arguments of the Watchtower Society for being a part of the NGO and see if they are valid.

Argument number one: "The reason why the Watchtower Society associated with the DPI was that the society needed to use the United Nations' library for research material on health, social, environmental, population and ecological problems." Was this really true?

Argument number two: "The society had been using the UN library before 1991 without associating with DPI but after 1991 the Watchtower's access would have been denied from the UN library unless the Watchtower became 'associated' with DPI." Was this true?

In order to check out the explanation that the Watchtower Society gave for becoming a member of the NGO, a woman wrote to the UN library, and here is the reply she received.

The question was: "Has the criteria for getting a library pass to the United Nations changed?"
Reply:

> The procedure for a library pass is the following: the interested party needs to fill out an application form and supply a letter of recommendation in support of the research. If the needed material is not available in the UN depository library (the list of depository libraries is posted at: http://www.un.org/depts/dhl/deplib/countries/), the application is approved and sent to UN Security. UN Security checks the application and, if approval is granted, instructs the Pass Office to issue a library pass for the applicant.

> The issuance of a library pass is independent of NGO status or any other status. There has been no change in the library pass policy.

> Best regards,
> [Name]
> Senior Reference Librarian
> UN/SA Reference Desk
> United Nations Library, New York.

Thus the two reasons given by the Watchtower Society for becoming a member of the NGO are not valid. The criteria for becoming a member of the NGO was set in 1968 and has never been changed. At that time a group or individual did not need to be a member of the NGO in order to use the UN library. Also, there was no need to join the NGO just to be able to use the library, because even if a person could not get into the UN library, all of the same information was available at "UN depository libraries." There are at least five of these libraries in the New York City area, so the society could have freely gone to them and obtained the same information. The society did not tell the truth.

The Watchtower's connection with the UN went much deeper than it has admitted. Even before the society became an official member of the NGO affiliated with the United Nations, it began to change its tone towards the UN. An article on page 10 of the September 8, 1991, *Awake* convinced the UN that the WTS was changing sides:

> Jehovah's Witnesses firmly believe that the United Nations is going to play a major role in world events in the very near future. No doubt these developments will be very exciting. And the results will have a far-reaching impact on your life. We urge you to ask Jehovah's Witnesses in your neighborhood for more details on this matter. The Bible clearly paints a picture showing that the United Nations will very shortly be given power and authority. The UN will then do some very astonishing things that may well amaze you. And you will be thrilled to learn that there is yet a better way near at hand that will surely bring eternal peace and security.

After the Watchtower Society became a member of the NGO, there were quite a few articles in the Watchtower publications that spoke favorably about the UN. These articles include *Awake* April 8, 1998, page 7; November 22, 1998, page 8; January 8, 1999, page 3; June 8, 1999, page 4; December 8, 2000, page 6–7; July 22, 2001, page 3; and *Watchtower* April 15, 1999, page 32. Most significant is a favorable article in the 11/8/1998 *Awake*, pages 6–7. This issue was submitted to the United Nations by the Watchtower Society and is listed on the UNCHR website along with many other NGO supporters of the UN. This article praised the UN's Commission on Human Rights.

There were other major changes by the Watchtower Society after it joined the NGO that indicated a change in attitude toward the UN and a desire to look more favorable. For instance, (1) The society lowered the punishment for belonging to a political party from disfellowshipping to disassociation. (2) In 1996 the society's prohibition against alternate service in place of military service was moderated to an issue of conscience. In fact, it went so far as to allow Witnesses in countries that do not permit alternate service to go into the military if drafted.

What is the bottom line? Official UN documents show that NGO membership is not and never was a requirement for using the UN library; there was no change in policy in 1991–92. This is just another example of the Watchtower Society writing one thing in its magazines and doing something different in secret—and then fabricating an excuse when caught.

How to Obtain Documentation

I have read many Watchtower books and magazines. As a result, I have on file copies from these publications on many different subjects. I would be more than willing to share this information with anyone who has questions or would like to continue investigating.

I have one packet of 130 pages on thirty different subjects concerning the Watchtower Society's false prophecies and its many changes in doctrine and practices. The packet is available for $15.00 plus $6.00 postage. You can contact me at:

6-B Swift Lane,
Whiting, NJ 08759-2922

732-350-0735

heleneast777@aol.com

This book was produced by CLC Publications. We hope it has been life-changing and has given you a fresh experience of God through the work of the Holy Spirit. CLC Publications is an outreach of CLC Ministries International, a global literature mission with work in over 50 countries. If you would like to know more about us or are interested in opportunities to serve with a faith mission, we invite you to contact us at:

CLC Ministries International
P.O. Box 1449
Fort Washington, PA 19034

Phone: (215) 542-1242
E-mail: orders@clcpublications.com
Website: www.clcpublications.com

- -

DO YOU LOVE GOOD CHRISTIAN BOOKS?
Do you have a heart for worldwide missions?

You can receive a FREE subscription to *HeartBeat*, CLC's newsletter on global literature missions.

Order by e-mail at:

clcheartbeat@clcusa.org

Or fill in the coupon below and mail to:

P.O. Box 1449
Fort Washington, PA 19034

FREE *HeartBeat* SUBSCRIPTION!

Name: _____

Address: _____

_____

Phone: _____   E-mail: _____

READ THE REMARKABLE STORY OF

the founding of
CLC INTERNATIONAL

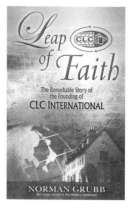

"Any who doubt that Elijah's God still lives ought to read of the money supplied when needed, the stores and houses provided, and the appearance of personnel in answer to prayer."
—Moody Monthly

Is it possible that the printing press, the editor's desk, the Christian bookstore and the mail order department can glow with the fast-moving drama of an "Acts of the Apostles"?

Find the answer as you are carried from two people in an upstairs bookroom to a worldwide chain of Christian bookcenters—multiplied by nothing but a "shoestring" of faith and by committed, though unlikely, lives.

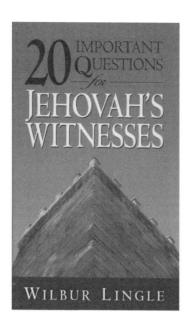

20 Important Questions for
Jehovah's Witnesses
Wilbur Lingle

Perhaps you are studying with a Jehovah's Witness at your home or maybe you just want to know more about what Witnesses believe. Here are 20 important questions for you to think seriously about.

Mass market, stapled • **28 pages**
978-0-87508-533-1